A SUN IN THE CLOUDS
AND OTHER ESSAYS

A SUN IN THE CLOUDS
AND OTHER ESSAYS

Alejo L. Villanueva, Jr.

New Day Publishers
Quezon City
1992

Copyright, 1992, by ALEJO L. VILLANUEVA, JR.
and NEW DAY PUBLISHERS
11 Lands St., VASRA/
P.O. Box 167, 1100 Quezon City, Philippines
Tel. No.: 99-80-46

All rights reserved.

Cover Design: Manny Gonzales

ISBN 971-10-0472-0

FOREWORD

IT is a tribute to the open-mindedness of Professor Villanueva that he asked me to write a foreword to his latest book, a collection of essays originally written for the *Philippine Daily Globe*. He knows that I, as a journalist and friend, do not agree with some of his thoughts about contemporary leaders and events, although he also knows that I agree with a good many of his ideas about freedom, democracy, and a better tomorrow for our country and people.

Reading through his essays provides a look at Filipino society through the clear prism of one who intensely, and passionately, believes in its bright future. The essays cover a wide ground, touching on such diverse subjects as history, politics, sociology, philosophy, management, communications, productivity, cooperativism, organizational development, and more.

Each one of them evokes optimism, a sense of national pride, a concern for unity, a need for perspective. The pieces on Banawe, EDSA, Panguil Bay, Marikina, Parañaque, probe into what is good, true, and beautiful about the Filipino. You can discern in them what one may well describe as the footprints of the creative spirit of the Filipino.

There are a good many other points of interest in his book that are refreshing and remarkably in accordance with my own observations about the future of our race and nation.

But for me, their one great virtue for today is that they alert the thoughtful reader to a wariness of those in our midst, especially the ones who wield tremendous political, economic and spiritual power, who would lead us astray with their mindless policies and horrendous mistakes, who would bog us down in semantics, arrogance, confusion, and just plain silliness, who would deprive us of this one opportune chance to grasp the bright future within our reach.

There is indeed one unifying theme running through Professor Villanueva's essays. And who better to lead us to them than one who truly sees, and hopes that we also can, the "sun in the clouds"?

NESTOR MATA

ACKNOWLEDGMENTS

I wish to convey my special thanks to the *Philippine Daily Globe* for granting permission to have a number of my essays in "From A Thoughtful Executive" included in this collection.

I am equally grateful to Dean Alfredo Tengco for his sustained encouragement.

The enriching dialogues with Nestor Mata helped crystallize some of my thoughts.

All those sessions with students of Social Philosophy at the Ateneo Graduate School of Business over the years raised questions which these essays try to answer.

Alejo L. Villanueva, Jr.

*To Justin Robert, Juan Miguel
and Carlos Francis . . .*

*For whom there will always be
a sun somewhere
in the clouds.*

CONTENTS

Foreword by Nestor Mata, v
Acknowledgments, vii

Gift from the Past, 1
    Back to Basics, 3
    Bayanihan Revisited, 4
    Banaue at the Crossroads, 8

The Ennobling Factor, 11
    Wanted: A Transformative Vision, 13
    The Evolution of Corporate Philosophy, 18
    The Anatomy of a Vision, 22
    The Substance of Value Formation, 23

Dynamics of Greatness, 27
    Memories of EDSA, 29
    The Soul of Giving, 31
    The San Dionisio Experience, 33

Beyond Corporate Walls, 37
    Humanities for Management, 39
    Corporate Democracy, 42
    PR in a Changing Milieu, 43
    A Closer Look at Image Engineering, 46
    Is There a Universal Manager?, 48

Questions from the Future, 51
    Whereto?, 53
    The Search for New Heroes, 55
    In Search of the Critical Mass, 58

Building Blocks for Tomorrow, 61
    Institution Building, 63
    The Government as an Organization, 65
    Loyalty to the Constitution, 67
    Democracy's Reason for Being, 69
    Towards Greater Productivity, 71

A New Beginning, 77
    Bright Notes, 79
    A Reason for Hope, 80
    A Sun in the Clouds, 83
    A Garden in Marikina, 85
    A Quiet Transformation, 87
    The Future for Farmers, 88

GIFT FROM THE PAST

BACK TO BASICS

TIME seems to stop moving at all in Batanes, a place that has so much to say about what living is all about.

This northernmost province is too far removed from the seat of political and economic power to be bothered by what the natives may consider as inconsequential things. By provincial standards, the people are too few. Compared to other provincial capitals, Basco does not have the usual amenities. One can literally count with his fingers the number of motorized vehicles in so rustic a landscape.

The sky and the sea are so overwhelming in their presence that one of cosmopolitan upbringing cannot help feeling a humbling sense of finitude. The serenity enables nature to make its gentle whispers to human ears.

In a place where life's concerns are so essentially basic, there is hardly any room for pride, ambition, and unnecessary acquisitions. What is there to be proud of when nature is often harsh with the weather? Why aim for fame and glory in a community that makes an unspoken religion out of brotherhood? Why be overly acquisitive when there is nothing much to spend one's wealth on? Why take one's self seriously when everybody else has been tempered by the seasons?

All these musings are elicited by the utter simplicity of Batanes and its gentle people. What the place lacks in the sophistication of modern life is more than amply compensated by its unaffected ways. When the hours of the day can be compared to the stages of the Divine Office etched in the hearts of dedicated missionaries, a life of communion with the Creator is as natural as breathing. Every little gesture becomes an act of prayer.

Batanes says something about the wisdom from the past, of lost horizons, and moments of innocence. There is no pressure to be more than what one already is. For the place is a reminder of man's transcendent beginning and end.

There is something too about Batanes that is very humanizing. The absolute dependence on the kindness of nature makes people equally kind and trusting. One is never a stranger. Hospitality is transparently authentic.

From the fast track of Makati, Batanes appears too remote and unreal. To anybody who is task-oriented, time conscious and agenda focused, Batanes is a very strange world. According to the measurable standards of development, the place is simply behind the times.

But in a larger sense, backwardness or progress is a matter of perspective. If life in a metropolis means pollution, traffic congestion, water shortage, power failure, urban blight, and peace and order problem, then it is not as progressive as it should be.

Urban dwellers may have forgotten something in pursuit of greater economic blessings. Batanes can provide some insights that are worth remembering.

BAYANIHAN REVISITED

MENTION of the term *bayanihan* often evokes the image of a house being carried on the shoulders of the able-bodied men of a community for transfer to a new location. The reality behind the image may not have become part of the childhood memories of many. It is even doubtful whether the Filipino youth of today and the generations that will come after will ever witness such an unaffected demonstration of community fellowship when both time and space are getting to be too far removed from a life of a simple vision, faith and love. The urbanization of society and the arrival of the life-style and the mindset of the future, with computers and fast-track activities are pushing the image of bayanihan even farther back into the distant past when caring for another was as natural as being entertained at night by the stars.

Perhaps it would be worth freezing the image or to hold it still like a frame on a video monitor. What is there in that familiar image associated with bayanihan? What is significant about a house being moved elsewhere through the efforts of many?

On the surface, what is perceived is just the physical process of transferring something. The weight of the object naturally requires combining various individual strengths. But the spirit that makes the whole process possible and desirable is something that goes beyond physics and mechanics. What any house in a small pastoral village means to ordinary people is something that indifferent bystanders may not be able to appreciate. To those who view the mobilization of manpower in terms of actual labor costs, the voluntary character of the whole bayanihan may not make much sense. Even Maslow's theory of motivation cannot adequately explain why people in a community share something of themselves to lighten the load of another. The logic of sharing which is so fundamentally human cannot be explained in terms of a mechanistic stimulus-response category. As true of things universal, what is essential is invisible to the eye.

There is something more to the image than meets the eye. The house is home to the family that owns it. To the father, the house is his legacy to those he loves. It is a sanctuary from the toils of the day. From it radiates so much peace, love and joy. Thus, when the house is relocated, it is not just a physical structure that is involved but the vessel of so much that a person gently treasures. When a neighbor or a relative or a friend volunteers to help in the relocation work, he makes an unconditional offer. He commits to share the burden. He cares. Because the owner of the house is never a stranger.

Think of the people involved in bayanihan. It must be comforting for anyone of them to be assured of the community's willingness and readiness to extend too many concerned shoulders should his own personal burden prove too heavy for his physical endurance. In such a situation, one becomes not just a being in the world or a shadow in a faceless crowd but a person-with-and-for-others. In a community where there are too many helping hands, one need not experience the pain of being alone. One can grow to the limits of his potentials because others who care are generous with their presence and their time.

Bayanihan also suggests that when there are enough people who are committed to help, a critical mass is reached when it becomes possible to lift any burden, solve any problem. Such a sense of an indivisible community, of finding strength in oneness and of discovering personal fulfillment in brotherhood with others must have been the moving spirit behind the birth of human society. So much trust and a subordination of the self to the greater good of a bigger human totality would be necessary for any individual to survive and grow. Isolation frustrates the human need to belong. Indeed, no man is an island. The death of any man is a diminution of the fabric of humanity.

Something transcendent is implied in the idea of bayanihan. For the decision to respond to the appeal of others for help, the choice of saying *yes* to someone in need is so universal and so timeless that it goes beyond the boundaries of religion, race or ideology. Thus, the global concern for the victims of the recent earthquake in Armenia is as Christian as it is Jewish or Islamic or Buddhist. The outpouring of sympathies for those who suffer from natural or man-made tragedies is but the noble stirring of man's compassion for a brother. It is as if bayanihan has been projected on a planetary scale. The simple village origin of bayanihan is echoed in the world that has evolved into a global village. By overcoming walls of mistrust and isolation, mankind has turned full circle in its quest for its divine beginning. The opening of doors and windows to the other members of the human community, the momentum towards peace, the international movement to save the planet Earth—all these do not happen by chance. They are the conscious articulation of converging minds and hearts infused with a redeeming vision that the survival of *homo sapiens* which is an endangered species lies in working together in harmony.

For all its universal message, bayanihan when seen in the context of a particular time and a specific place is culture bound. Bayanihan as it has developed in the Philippines carried an imprint of the positive Filipino character that has been formed over the years. Its cradle was the early *barangay*, a small social unit, a clan composed of about 50 families that were presumably interrelated. The barangay was a self-contained village with its own leader who functioned more as the head of an extended family. Within its sphere of governance the interest of the village would always prevail. The concept of self or the sense of individualism was not as evident as it was in the Old World at the time of the Copernican Revolution. The identity of the individual member of the barangay was subsumed by the clan. One could not be other than an integral part of his clan. It was, therefore, unthinkable for any member of the barangay to be selfish. His life was intertwined with the village.

Given a community-oriented social structure, a philosophy of life developed that would put primacy on living and working together. And inasmuch as the survival of the barangay would depend on the harmonious interaction among its members, the values of *pagmamalasakit, pagdadamayan, pagbibigayan, pagtutulungan, kagandahang loob* and *kababaang loob,* among others, would be emphasized, reinforced and internalized. The barangay had a psychosocial mechanism in terms of shared values for insuring its continuity.

The values that originated in the barangay became the underpinnings of the practice of bayanihan. Doing something for somebody was not just an act of moral duty. It was the fulfillment of one's nature as an inseparable part of a community of brothers.

From its cultural presuppositions, the logic behind the etymology of bayanihan becomes clear. Bayanihan puts the interest and welfare of the *bayan* above everything else. If this is what patriotism is all about, then this virtue is historically rooted in the character of the Filipino. There were too many events in the country's history that demonstrated a faithful adherence to the ideal of yielding to the call of the bayan.

A person who subordinates his own interests to the higher good of the bayan is a *bayani* or hero. And the whole process whereby a bayani multiplies himself in the act of doing his very best for the sake of the bayan is bayanihan.

Thus, the image of a house being borne on the shoulders of men in a village is just a symbol, however familiar, of the spirit of bayanihan. There have been other manifestations. There can be more contemporary expressions.

Bayanihan was there when hundreds of sunburned bodies toiled patiently for years to catch the rain from the clouds by carving rice terraces on the mountains of Banaue. It was there with Rizal and Del Pilar and the rest of the Propaganda Movement in Spain as they consecrated their talents to defend the honor of their motherland. It was there with Bonifacio as he selflessly organized the Katipunan in a span of four years into a secret fraternity of 30,000 idealistic soldiers of the revolution. It was there in the foxholes of Bataan and the tunnel of Corregidor. It is there now among Filipino doctors in the United States who keep on sending medical missions to the Philippine hinterlands. And it is there too among hundreds of thousands of Filipino workers overseas whose sweat, toils, and tears help support the nation's economy.

Bayanihan need not be dramatic. It can be an intangible quality in the soul of every living institution human enough to care. It can be the simple idea behind the words of a corporate philosophy. It can be in the quiet obsession of an enterpreneur to place his energies and resources in the service of society. It can be in the corporate attitude and practice of genuinely caring for the good of people. It can be in one man's overriding vision to do more for others. Or it can also be in the collective enthusiasm to strive for excellence and to find more and better ways to serve society's ends.

In the heart of someone inspired by the spirit of bayanihan, a gentle bell keeps on ringing: *"Walang sinuman ang nabubuhay para sa sarili lamang."*

BANAUE AT THE CROSSROADS

A visual experience of the world-famous Banaue Rice Terraces from the heights of the pine-scented Viewpoint inevitably evokes a sense of awe. One is rendered speechless imagining how a cluster of majestic mountains could allow themselves to be sculptured by human hands into an architecture of beauty and function, of scaling rice paddies which to a prayerful mind seem like a stairway to the sky.

It was as if Nature in its patient yearning for the touch of the human spirit finally yielded in the fullness of time to the transformative power of creative Man. Banaue is a unique monument to the constructive relationship between Man and Nature, to the harmony between the ancient reverential respect for natural things and the earth's generous response to basic human needs. The architects of Banaue's Rice Terraces were surely not strangers to the divine message: *"Be fruitful and multiply and replenish the earth.*" These words seem to be echoed unceasingly by the mountain winds.

The grandeur that is Banaue is a world in itself where time's movement is felt in the alternation of night and day. Perish the thought of a digital watch or a Daylight Saving Time. Where Nature prevails as an omnipresent timekeeper, moments and seconds lose their fleeting beats. In the time horizon of the mountains, there is no space for the fast track. One grows with the seasons and learns intimately that life is a cycle of birth and death. One need not fear surrendering the dreams of youth for where living is intertwined with nature, life becomes a continuum with no fixed compartments but with interrelated stages of the process of maturation.

Banaue is not just a return to the time of simple joy, of solitude in communion, of fresh air and cool mountain spring. It is a refreshing reminder of a people's capacity for greatness. It is a mirror of an ideal national character.

Even by present standards, the rice terraces of Banaue can never be accomplished without a collective spirit, a sense of mission, direction and organization. If today's planners, architects, engineers, finance men and other technocrats were to undertake a project of the nature and magnitude of the rice terraces, the task alone would be so overwhelming that the initial reaction would be—"It can't be done!" The maze of bureaucracy alone would defy even the decisive exercise of political will at the highest level. An inter-agency coordinating body would have to be created. Feasibility studies would have to be prepared. Consultants from various disciplines would have to be engaged. With all these and more, there is no certainty that the project as planned could be finished in time. It is possible (and it is likely based on contemporary experience) that in midstream the project may be adversely affected by any media criticism coming from a dissatisfied sectoral group.

For all their primitive ways, the ancient builders of the rice terraces as moved by the need to survive had only their native talents, patience, perseverance and industry to rely on. There was no help coming from any external group. With bare hands and crude tools, the builders created rice paddies on the sides of the mountains. Day after day. Year after year. Generation after generation. Until finally the finished handiwork of a simple people working in unison and driven by a common vision was unveiled.

There is no written record of the names of all those who took part in one of the world's remarkable construction undertakings. It is just as well. And it does not really matter anymore. For in the anonymity of those great builders lies the immortality of their legacy to the nation that needs a rekindling of their spirit for it to endure.

Surely, the Banaue Rice Terraces as portrayed in souvenir cards serve as the country's premier tourist attraction. But there is much more to the scenic wonder than what the eyes can see. Banaue together with *La Solidaridad, Noli Me Tangere, El Filibusterismo,* the Katipunan, the Philippine Flag, the Philippine National Anthem and the *Panatang Makabayan* says something eloquently about the greatness in the Filipino.

THE ENNOBLING FACTOR

WANTED: A TRANSFORMATIVE VISION

DECADENCE has been the fate of many living organisms.

This phenomenon has not spared societies, governments, and business organizations. Not even the great civilizations of the past were strong enough to neutralize the seemingly imperceptible intrusion of the early signs of decline.

In the case of prehistoric animals that had vanished aeons ago, there was admittedly a failure to adapt to drastic changes in the environment. It could be that their genetic code had not been programmed to produce a series of survival-oriented reactions.

Many ancient societies failed the test of time. They are now relics and artifacts from a distant past that could be reached only through the painstaking efforts of a few archaeologists.

A number of empires have become historical footnotes. Rome. Gran Brittania. The Rising Sun. They were overtaken by events and forces they failed to understand.

Time was when the sun was always up in the British Empire, when all of South America was under Iberia, when the western world shared the same communion and followed a common liturgy, when the tempo of life was attuned to the rhythmic pulse of nature, when there was something apparently enduring to hold on to, when both leaders and followers were comforted by the thought that man was the center of the universe. But that age of chivalry, of the guild system and monasticism had since disappeared. After the Copernican Revolution, things were never the same again.

Rulers were overthrown. Political systems were supplanted. Governments were short-lived. All because of an acute insensitivity, a common failure to deal constructively with new realities within their sphere of governance.

The business world too has its history of tragic mistakes. The collapse of monopolies, corporate bankruptcies, products that the market rejected, service offerings that became irrelevant, expansions and diversifications that had more daring than purpose, sellouts and mergers not animated by a genuine concern for people or a higher moral purpose. The crash of 1929 with dire consequences could repeat itself. It almost did in October 1987.

Those who preferred to bask in the unrepeatable glory of their past were all left behind. Equally bypassed by time's passing were those who did not care to see far enough, who did not have the courage to look beyond. To them the echoes of previous victories were intoxicating. Grappling with the uncertainties of the future was unsettling.

An underlying cause to explain the irrelevance or decline of any institution or organization could be the lack of a capacity for imagination and the willingness to pursue a dream or its realization. Perhaps what really matters is not so much the fulfillment of a dream which happens at a fixed point in time but the very process of dreaming in itself. It is the spirit of the dreamer that gives a unique form to a shapeless mass. It is the presence of a vision that opens windows to the winds of change. The visionary blazes new trails, finds alternative pathways and discovers fresh horizons.

Without a synthesizing vision, the velocity of change that is sweeping through the world today could be confusing, disorienting and even threatening. The many breakthroughs in science and technology with an expanding list of applications, the shifts in cultural perspectives, the tremendous explosion of knowledge and the many transformations taking place in every significant area of human activity—all these would just be a cluster of meaningless impressions unless there is a central vision to give coherence, purpose and direction.

It was the vision of Washington that served as the initial foundation of the American republic precisely at a time when the newly liberated 13 colonies could have chosen a monarchical system had the father of the United States been so self-seeking. When it was very unpopular and downright divisive to speak of abolishing the institution of slavery, Lincoln did not waver in his noble mission to spread the gospel of racial equality even at the risk of a civil war. Lincoln's vision saved the Union.

Other great leaders in another time discerned in the devastation wrought by the destructive side of man a rare opportunity to build the underpinnings of a peaceful future. The United Nations is the child of the collective vision of the leaders of the Allied Powers *to save succeeding generations from the scourge of war.*

The Filipino nation has never been wanting in this most vital gift. As far back as the generation of Rizal and Bonifacio, the vision of national unity, freedom and prosperity was a popular concern. That overriding passion for self-rule and the consciousness of sharing a common past and of living together in a state of bondage ignited the first nationalist revolution in Asia that eventually formed the first Asian democratic republic. The generation of Osmeña, Quezon, Laurel and Recto inherited that vision.

A much younger leader who could very well empathize with ordinary people and, therefore, read their sentiments and articulate their aspirations was Ramon Magsaysay. His vision was simple—*a government for the people*. He gave it flesh and blood. He transformed it into a tangible fact with his heart and soul. It was one great ideal subsequently betrayed by the forces of tyranny and hypocrisy.

During the dark days of the dictatorship, one man stood out in the midst of a cowering population to keep the dream of democracy alive. Benigno S. Aquino, Jr. held tight to his uncompromising vision of helping rekindle the flame of freedom in his country. In the process he defied the windmills of oppression and became a true martyr to so great a cause. That vision was crystallized by the blood of its foremost believer. Until it was so overpowering that an entire nation found the courage to break its chains.

Just as necessity is the mother of invention, diversity is the cradle of vision. The intolerance and despotism of the Medieval Age led to a radical reexamination of the basis of political power and a rethinking of the nature of man's institutionalized relationship with God. The excesses of the Industrial Revolution prompted Karl Marx to go to England to make an in-depth study of the capitalist system. In one of those quiet moments in the British Museum while Marx was reflecting on the miseries of the factory workers as reported by the Factory Inquiry Commission, the beginning of a communist vision took shape.

Defeats transformed the vanquished Germans and Japanese into economic miracles. From the ruins of Frankfurt, Hamburg, Munich, Bremen, Stuttgart, Dusseldorf, Tokyo, Nagoya, Yokohama, Kobe, Hiroshima and Nagasaki emerged new landscapes of unprecedented progress. But the real miracle is not in the strength of the yen or the deutsche mark. The remarkable rebirth of Germany and Japan began with an uncompromising vision to move forward.

Such a strong predisposition to accept courageously the challenges of the future could explain the phenomenon of the "tiger economies" of the East, the NIC's Singapore, South Korea, Taiwan and Hong Kong. Each of the leaders of these economies was imbued with an overriding vision to improve the quality of life of the people. Each pursued that vision with total zeal to a point that what began as a leader's dream became a national obsession.

In the world of business, the corporate vision is almost always originated and shaped by the man at the helm who has a fundamental and clear grasp of the nature of the business of his organization, its essentials, its potentials and its relationships. The classic Model T that revolutionized car manufacturing was a spark from the vision of a leading captain of American industry, Henry Ford.

Out of a corporate philosophy that deeply values excellence is the international legend of IBM. IBM's position of leadership in computers is traceable to the vision of its founder, Mr. Thomas J. Watson, Sr., who succeeded in inspiring his people to *THINK* always.

Something as essentially American as Disneyland was but a dream in the mind of the world's most celebrated dreamer who made a great fortune by selling fantasies. As Walt Disney said, "If you can dream it, you can do it."

San Miguel Corporation's primacy in Philippine industry with its diversified operations was fixed in the mind of its grand old man, the late Don Andres Soriano.

Who would have thought that the Makati grassland on both sides of the old Highway 54 were to be transformed into high-class residential subdivisions, commercial complexes, hotels, high-rise condominiums and office buildings? But to Col. Joseph McMicking, a land development visionary, there were intimations of a modern skyline even among weeds and swamps.

Irrespective of the nature of an organization, the formation of its vision is a function of leadership. Its propagation is also the leader's main responsibility. But in the dissemination of a vision, in making it an organizational ideal the leader needs a managerial perspective and a grasp of organizational realities.

So that a vision may have the right focus for managing change, the leader should be able to integrate it with the key elements of the organization, i.e., strategy, structure, systems, staff, skills, style and superordinate goals. To do this, there is a need to know the organization's readiness to share the leader's vision and its capacity to renew itself. Some questions may be of help. For instance, does the organization have a planning discipline to prepare for the future? Is there a sense of mission? Is there any blueprint for dealing with changes in the environment?

Does the network of relationships allow for smooth organizational shifts? Does the configuration of roles encourage innovation? Is the atmosphere conducive to a cross-fertilization of insights?

Is there sufficient flexibility in rules and procedures so that new ways of doing things and of getting things done are permitted? Are the people of the organization of such a background and training that they are always attuned to new possibilities? Are they capable of critical reflection and are they comfortable with it?

Is creativity a valued skill? Are the available competences limited to purely technical matters? Is the organization's way of thinking and doing tradition-bound? Or is it tolerant of ambiguities and uncertainties?

Does the organizational culture contain something transcendent and spiritual? Is there a nobility of purpose in the entire value system? Is there a pervading philosophy that inspires enthusiasm and commitment?

It is not enough, however, to have vision in general. For vision to be meaningful and useful, it must inspire and transform. For one can have a vision and yet not see enough. One can see far and yet miss what is immediate. One can look back only to find faint images. One can take note of the present and still lose sight of its nuances and implications. Or one can try to look into the future and find nothing but uncertainties.

A transformative vision has an integrated sense of the past, the present and the future. It has enough hindsight to find wisdom in the lessons of previous mistakes and successes. It has enough insight to discern the significance of the moment and its unrepeatability. It has enough foresight to see new opportunities even in an unknown future.

A vision can transform a nation or an organization only when it is pursued with passion and intensity. Those immortal names who contributed to mankind's progress and even those who are breaking new grounds in many disciplines have one thing in common —stretching the limits of what is possible. There is a sense of childlike wonder, the never-ending enthusiasm to ask *why not?*

Nothing frustrates the presence of a vision more than the lack of a sensitivity to a world of possibilities, the blind accommodation with the *status quo* or the absence of critical reflection. Indeed, narrow-mindedness, manuals and bureaucracies are the enemies of visionaries.

It would be tragic if a dream were just kept in the heart and mind of its dreamer. A vision has to be shared. It must be communicated. But to be accepted, the originator of the vision has to be highly credible. The vision has to be simple. It must be perceived through the authentic testimony of its author as reflected in every little word and even in an insignificant deed.

But once a vision is accepted, it has to be sustained and nourished through reaffirmations and rituals. Until the spirit that gave birth to it goes tired and weary. Or until a better vision comes along.

THE EVOLUTION OF CORPORATE PHILOSOPHY

A survey of the world's successful corporations indicates an emerging trend in the direction of corporate thinking. There is a growing appreciation within the corporate world of the relevance of certain intangible realities that are traditionally within the immediate competence of humanists, philosophers and men of letters. Corporate philosophies especially in enlightened business circles have become as important as corporate strategies.

Why is there great corporate interest now in such unquantifiable factors as philosophies, values and beliefs? Why must the pragmatic discipline of business which is normally concerned only with the bottomline, cashflow, profit maximization and ROI open itself to the abstractions of metaphysics?

Was there not a time too long ago when the prevailing thinking along corporate corridors was—*business is business*? The primary focus on purely economic considerations underscored this outlook. Limiting the CEO position to a finance, production or marketing man reinforced it even more. Whoever heard of a philosophy man or a humanities graduate making it to the top of the executive ladder? Sure, a theology major or even an ex-priest would not be totally unqualified for employment in a bank or a manufacturing firm. But in the event he is hired, it is only because he may have demonstrated to the personnel people such skills as teaching or writing. And his assignment within the organization is invariably either with training or public information.

The "greening" of a philosophical consciousness in the corporate world was totally unthinkable in the early stages of the industrial age. In fact, the free mercantilist atmosphere that dominated Europe and the United States from the last quarter of the nineteenth century up to the post-World War II years glorified the so-called impersonal market forces in spite of the moral pleadings of the papal encyclicals *Rerum Novarum* (1891) and *Quadragesimo Anno* (1931) for a social conscience in economic affairs.

Even business or management education at its inception in the United States was silent about philosophical, moral and humanistic issues. The curricular offerings of the pioneering business schools were heavily influenced by Frederick Taylor's scientific management with its accent on productivity and time and motion efficiency. It was as if the human factor was just an expendable element in production until the captains of industry discovered through the famous Hawthorne experiment that the worker is much more than an efficient biological machine.

With the remarkable success stories of such organizational models as Japan Inc., IBM, Sony and Xerox, among others, a new dimension in management thinking was evolved. The case histories of these organizations have been analyzed extensively from a multidisciplinary perspective. There are those who would attribute institutional achievements to R & D efforts and far-reaching marketing networks. Others would single out the level of manpower competence and managerial expertise.

Other business establishments, however, have similar attributes. But somehow they fail to get closer to that exceptional class of excellent organizations such as IBM, Sony and Xerox. Where lies the difference? What do excellent organizations have in common which is lacking in others? I am highly inclined to think that the crucial variable is the presence of a unifying philosophy, a core of shared values, a sense of mission.

Behind the economic miracle that is Japan is the underlying collective vision of a nation to rise above the ruins of humiliating defeat and regain its dignity and glory. Behind the quality control circles of Toyota, Nissan, Nikon, Seiko, etc. is a pervasive attitude of walking the extra mile for the sake of the land of the rising sun.

The global IBM which is synonymous with computer is essentially a corporate philosophy in action—the unqualified and total pursuit of excellence.

These examples are illustrative of what corporate philosophy, properly internalized and applied, can do. A corporate vision may be an end in itself. But it is not precluded from having a positive effect on the bottomline in terms of its motivational value for people and its relevance to strategy formulation.

How is corporate philosophy shaped or developed? At this point, a fundamental distinction must be made between the text of an intended philosophy and the philosophy itself. It is just like saying that the musical notes cannot be equated with music. Words are not the same as poetry. Failure to understand this has its own pitfalls. Thus, the PR department of a publicity-seeking firm may engage the services of a wordsmith to craft the language of a proposed corporate creed. The finished product may be engraved in bronze and displayed prominently at the lobby of a firm's head office. It may be included in all institutional communications such as brochures and annual reports. But the whole process does not necessarily lead to the formulation of a corporate philosophy.

What can make the whole effort a meaningless exercise is if it is undertaken purely in the context of image building. Corporate philosophy is then merely an afterthought and never a natural articulation of an incipient vision. Sooner or later, the pseudo-philosophy will be unmasked by the discerning public for what it is really worth—gimmickry.

It is not too uncommon to know of corporate philosophies emanating from the chairman or the chief executive officer. In very rare cases, the corporate creed as articulated by the corporate leadership gets institutionalized because it happens to reflect the aspirations of those below. But where there is no congruence between the respective ideals of the leader and the followers, the philosophy prescribed does not become the credo of the organization. A set of values cannot be legislated. A given way of thinking and behaving can only be promoted with patience and consistency among its possible acceptors. And this suggests that everybody within the organization must have a part in the formulation of its philosophy. For nobody is so insignificant that he has no vision of his own to share.

Guided by these thoughts, the people of Home Development Mutual Fund (Pag-IBIG) saw the need to redefine their institutional mission and review their corporate ideals in the light of the principle of public accountability and in view of the voluntary nature of Pag-IBIG membership. Thus, they set into motion the process of institutionalized regional multisectoral consultations with Pag-IBIG members—the government employees, private employees, factory workers, employers and even representatives of companies completely out of Pag-IBIG. Inasmuch as the members really own Pag-IBIG, their presence in consultation meetings initiated by Pag-IBIG management was requested. They were cooperative in giving an objective assessment of Pag-IBIG's past directions and policies. They also shared their views on Pag- IBIG's prospective thrusts.

Pag-IBIG management received some negative feedback particularly on the wide gap between the housing requirements of members and Pag-IBIG's actual deliveries. Also given were new insights into what Pag-IBIG ought to be. Indeed, it was the start of a continuing process of learning directly from the collective wisdom of Pag-IBIG members.

When an institution finally comes out with the formulation of its philosophy, this is just a beginning. For the corporate philosophy has yet to be verified and validated through the public thoughts and acts of its conceptualizers, articulators and promoters. Any variance between corporate creed and corporate behavior will be a hindrance to the internalization of the philosophy.

As an old Chinese philosopher once taught: "When a man says something, I listen to his words and then I watch for his deeds."

THE ANATOMY OF A VISION

A democratic order is necessarily mandated to give top priority attention to the welfare of the large majority. In the country today, democracy's largest constituency consists of farmers and fishermen.

The question, therefore, is—what can democracy offer to the majority of the Filipino people? What is in it for the sons and daughters of the soil and the sea?

Many practical answers can be given. In fact concrete measures were conceived and adopted in the past in an attempt to help the agricultural sector. Several action programs were implemented for the same reason. The Masagana 99. The cattle dispersal project. The Biyayang Dagat plan. And many more.

What seems lacking in all these interventions is an integrating vision, an underlying philosophy that relates all the bits and pieces to a coherent whole.

In response to this need, an envisioning process has been initiated at the Department of Agriculture. The institutional vision speaks of *dynamic agro-industrial communities thriving with a new breed of farmer-entrepreneurs.*

Given this vision, what supplementary values are needed to give it force, substance, form and application? Unless this dream is promoted, discussed, reflected on and internalized in the entire implementing organization, nothing much can be achieved.

It is not enough to have a vision. The organization must try to look inward and assess its willingness as well as its ability to pursue a given ideal to its realization. How equipped is the organization to be an effective catalyst of change?

Is the organizational structure supportive of the vision? Are the functions and relationships so well defined such that coordination is enhanced? Is there a clear, coherent and workable strategy? Are systems results-oriented? Are members of the staff trained, motivated and united? Are there adequate skills for maximizing resources, for getting things done, for patient attention to details? Is the style of performance premised on a great sense of urgency? Are there shared values of *pagmamalasakit* and *pagbibigayan*?

These questions into organizational capabilities are raised to focus on the practical aspect of realizing a vision. There is, however, a more basic issue—the need for a sense of mission to get the vision through. This means that anybody who believes in a vision is imbued with a missionary zeal to make his dream come true.

In another time in different places, there were visionaries who thought of things that never were and asked, "Why not?" Their unshakeable faith in the power of their dream has since given so much meaning to man's fragile existence.

THE SUBSTANCE OF VALUE FORMATION

SOMETIME ago, an employee of a local subsidiary of a multinational drug company had to be hospitalized for an extended period due to an expensive illness. At the end of his confinement, the total hospital bill consisting of doctors' fees, medicines, laboratory examinations, room, etc. added up to a prohibitive amount.

Expectedly, the subsidiary has a generous staff hospitalization program. But even this was not sufficient to cover the entire cost of this single confinement case. Under the company's policy, the employee referred to had to shoulder personally that portion of the bill in excess of the program's coverage. There was a big difference which stood at six figures. The employee did not have the personal resources with which to pay his share of the bill.

The officer in charge of personnel administration referred the problem to the chief executive officer who decided that the company should bear the full cost of the employee's hospitalization. And the reason of the top man was simple: "This is one way to substantiate our corporate philosophy that we truly care about our people."

Obviously, the decision to pick up the tab exceeded standard policy parameters. Some would call it, from the standpoint of a cost-conscious benefits administration, as the beginning of an unaffordable corporate paternalism. Others might think of it as a charitable act which does not really belong to a profit-oriented business organization. Similarly there are those who would question the logic of the decision in terms of its effect on the bottomline.

Whether the decision was logical or emotional, calculated or impulsive, the effect on the beneficiary, the immediate members of his family, his friends and fellow employees was beyond quantification. The employee concerned was moved to tears. It never entered his mind that the company which he had joined at its inception would be too humane to give him a caring hand at a time when he needed it most. No other gesture of corporate compassion could have been more eloquent.

So much about this case revolved around the chief executive officer, his own humanistic values as a manager, his professional training, and his warm unassuming personality. A man of few words, he is able to get things done through and with the enthusiastic cooperation of the people he works with. There is something so distinctly authentic about just the way he is, the way he talks, walks, smiles and presides over meetings. He is totally unaffected that even a stranger would feel comfortable in his presence. No sign of external sophistication one would ordinarily associate with the leader of a modern and profitable pharmaceutical firm.

This exceptional executive who had a rural upbringing in one of the remote towns of the Visayas and who has an MBA from a leading management training institution may not realize it—but he has something useful to share with the management profession. And that is—the *dynamics of value formation and dissemination.* Deep in his heart he cares about people. He is really *matulungin* (helpful), *mapagbigay* (accommodating), and *maunawain* (understanding). This is his character. And yet his people orientation does not run counter to his task orientation. The fact is—he has ably steered the company he had set up from a humble beginning to what it is today. He has chalked up an impressive profit performance with the active involvement of a highly inspired work force.

Nobody in his organization ever doubts the truth of the institutional value of *pagmamalasakit* (caring). There have been a number of executive decisions and corporate acts that all combine to give substance and meaning to this cherished ideal. That decision to pay the full cost of the hospital bill of the employee mentioned earlier was just one of them.

The beneficiary of that act of corporate compassion did not have to be told the meaning of pagmamalasakit. This particular value could have been played up in the corporate brochure or in the regular orientation program for new recruits. But all the verbalization means nothing unless its subject is personally experienced. Surely, action speaks louder than words. To the employee who was relieved of a heavy financial burden, the corporate pagmamalasakit is not an empty slogan. It is a living reality made all the more meaningful by the voluntary expression of corporate sensitivity. The corporate gesture was very well received because it was sincerely made.

As expected, the beneficiary developed a strong sense of gratitude to the company. The Filipino's natural *utang na loob* was touched. The chief executive officer's gesture has had a multiplier effect. The pagmamalasakit of the firm has earned the pagmamalasakit of its employees for its objectives.

One need not wonder, therefore, why in some corporations expressions of corporate generosity do not elicit appreciation from intended recipients. A package of employee benefits no matter how liberal does not necessarily become motivational forces. Some unionized employees feel, rightly or wrongly, that they have fought for these benefits in CBA negotiations and that these have been obtained as a matter of right. Management, however, feels otherwise and considers its benefits program as reflective of its benevolence. The two perceptions are poles apart.

Obviously, something is missing.

DYNAMICS OF GREATNESS

MEMORIES OF EDSA

EDSA brings back voices and images of what was perhaps the most spectacular political drama ever recorded by electronic broadcast journalism for millions of televiewers around the world. Memories of that sense of euphoria that came with the rebirth of Philippine democracy are too precious to leave behind.

There were many bits and pieces in the mosaic that was the February 1986 Revolution. One could focus on the spark ignited by the rebellious RAM. Or the sea of humanity that shielded the mutineers from loyalist troops. Or the helpless nuns kneeling before an army tank. Or those helicopter gunships descending at dawn on Camp Crame in support of the rebellion. Or the deafening cheers that greeted the downfall of an unwanted regime.

Behind those still frames or a video playback from the past was the soul of a nation reborn. EDSA was the handiwork of the Filipino who found the courage to win back his dignity and freedom at the risk of his life. For so noble a cause God could never have been far behind. EDSA was a watershed in the nation's history. It was the story of a nation coming to terms with itself.

It was the general perception then that EDSA was supposed to end tyranny, corruption, profligacy, and mismanagement of national affairs. Conversely, it was expected to usher in a new democratic order as a prelude to a period of political stability and economic recovery. It was also meant to mark the beginning of a process of national moral renewal.

After the celebration the real work began. A popular revolutionary government was installed. Suddenly there was a change in the nation's leadership without the benefit of a smooth transition. Understandably, the new leadership must first insure its own survival in the midst of all conceivable threats. Any apparatus perceived, rightly or wrongly, as contrary to the ideals of the revolutionary government was either dismantled or reconstituted. Thus, the Batasang Pambansa which was dominated by the party of the previous regime was dismantled. The composition of the Supreme Court was changed. The old fundamental law was replaced by the Freedom Constitution. The business interests of people closely identified with the deposed ruler were sequestered on the assumption that they had been illegally acquired.

At the local level, the revolutionary government placed its own OIC's in all provincial, city and municipal extensions down to the barangay in lieu of elected local officials who were perceived to be still part of the machinery of the past establishment.

It was a sweeping and sudden overhaul of political institutions in a determined move to consolidate power. It was all part of the dynamics of political transformation.

Lest it be regarded as drifting from its avowed democratic orientation, the revolutionary government allowed a wide expansion of democratic space. Newspapers have since proliferated. Political detainees were released and dialogues with insurgents and secessionists conducted in the name of national reconciliation. And attempts to break up state monopolies have been initiated.

The next item on the agenda was to take the high road back to full democracy. A Constitutional Commission was created to prepare a draft of a new fundamental law that would truly reflect popular sentiments. The draft was subsequently ratified in a nationwide plebiscite. The new Constitution is a categorical rejection of all the abusive practices of authoritarian rule. The presidential system has been revived. A bicameral legislature is back in place.

Then came the first democratic elections since 1971. The people chose their respective representatives and the members of the Senate. Later, local elections were held putting an end to the system of OIC's. Peaceful mechanisms for installing and removing public officials were set in place.

In a span of two years, the government that was created by direct popular intervention through a peaceful revolution succeeded in fully restoring democracy even against great odds. This was a distinct achievement in itself possibly unequalled in other countries that have also regained their freedom.

The rebirth of democracy is just the beginning. The real challenge of EDSA is how to achieve national reconstruction, reconciliation and moral regeneration within the context of a cherished democratic order.

EDSA is a vision. Its remembrance may help the nation see far and beyond.

THE SOUL OF GIVING

A famous charismatic bishop of Recife, Brazil once said that nobody is so poor that he has nothing to give. The truth of this statement was demonstrated as the little folks of Davao City—the tricycle drivers, the market vendors, the vegetable farmers, the security guards, the construction workers, etc. together with their more materially endowed fellow Davaweños gave birth to a collective philanthropic project. Out of a common dream of many concerned Davawenos, rich and poor, was formed the beginning of what is now the Davao Scholarship Trustfoundation, Inc.

Ordinarily, the mere mention of the word *foundation* right away evokes images of a Rockefeller, a Ford, a Carnegie or a Yangco, a Ventura, a Lopez, an Araneta, etc. Philanthropy is almost always associated with persons of wealth. A benefactor with substantial fortune is so moved by *noblesse oblige* that he sets aside an amount the earnings of which fund a predetermined humanitarian concern. In some cases, the heirs of a dead benefactor seek to honor his memory by setting up a foundation in his name.

But when we hear of ordinary people below the poverty line who choose to donate whatever they can afford to a foundation, we are somewhat surprised. Not that it is impossible. Or unrealistic. Or out of character. It is simply because the general impression is—that those who have less in life should be the beneficiary and not the benefactor.

A dentist from Davao City, however, thinks and insists otherwise. Dr. Ruben Angeles, the founder-president of the Davao

Scholarship Trustfoundation, Inc. has persistently defied the pressure of common opinion. He has always believed that the willingness to give is part of human nature, and as such, is not contingent on social or economic status.

Thus, when Dr. Angeles started the foundation in early 1983 with the premise that even the poor are potential donors, his immediate family and his friends had very serious doubts. When he went on an extensive personal selling campaign to gain a wide acceptance for his idea of a foundation, he was met with ridicule and indifference. There were even unkind remarks that he had run out of patients so that he had to set up a foundation in order to survive. All these he took in stride.

Almost seven years later, Dr. Angeles witnessed the realization of his dream. As of September 24, 1989, the fund of the Davao Scholarship Trustfoundation, Inc. stood at P471,455.86 which have been generated out of donations as small as P5.00 from Cristina Galus and as big as P50,000.00 from an anonymous donor. Since its inception, the foundation's income alone has provided scholarships to some 38 poor but deserving students who have all graduated from various schools in Davao City. These young beneficiaries of the foundation have become benefactors in their own right. Now that they are gainfully employed, they have donated some P15,000.00 to the foundation to support another student. Each donation that is freely given by a former beneficiary always marks a process of self-renewal for the foundation.

It is Dr. Angeles' refusal to make a qualitative distinction between "small" and "big" donations that must have attracted the ordinary people of Davao City to join his crusade. As he emphasizes now and then, any help in whatever quantity from anybody can mean so much to someone else. Like that blind fellow who wrote the foundation to ask for a scholarship so that someday he could be a teacher of the blind. It is not so much the quantifiable amount that truly matters but the depth of the conviction behind the act of giving.

Dr. Angeles may not realize it but the foundation that he has spearheaded has become something of an equalizer. Among the donors of the foundation, there is no air of condescension one could feel from the bigger benefactors in their attitude towards their smaller peers. Likewise, there is hardly a posture of inferiority from the smaller donors as they relate to the more affluent givers. They are all bound together by a unifying concern—to join forces so that diligent but financially handicapped students can get a college education.

What makes this unique experiment in multisectoral philanthropy all the more significant is the fact that Davao City is really a microcosm of the Philippines. This point of convergence for so many ethnic groups suggests future possibilities for the whole country. If Ilocanos, Cebuanos, Tagalogs, Ilongos, Maranaws, etc., Christians and Muslims, rich and poor, professionals and dropouts, employees and entrepreneurs can all join hands to provide educational opportunities to the less fortunate youth, then there is so much hope for the future of the nation.

What has been going on in Davao City for seven years is more than just the vision of one dentist and his friends. The Davao Scholarship Trustfoundation, Inc. is proof enough that we have many citizens who can rise, as in fact they have risen, above personal, sectoral, and ethnic interests.

The people of Davao City have lighted many little candles. They see no point in cursing the darkness.

THE SAN DIONISIO EXPERIENCE

MUCH has been said about the urgent need for greater national unity. Others underscore the primacy of a widespread envisioning process so that certain values are clarified, developed and disseminated. There are those who echo the constitutional ideal of people empowerment as a precondition to democratic development.

These theoretical musings somehow suggest Paolo Freire's rejection of "verbalism," i.e., preoccupation with reflection at the expense of action. But one wonders if indeed we are way beyond the reflective stage so that all that should follow is "action." But even on the level of action, the desired effects have yet to be perceived by the intended beneficiaries. What is ideal of course is a symmetry of reflection and action when thoughts get to be so crystallized as to cause their immediate realization.

How can serious reflection lead to meaningful action? Is there a paradigm? At the community level, there has been a continuing experiment that deserves a closer look because of its multiplier effect. The experience of the San Dionisio Credit Cooperative of Parañaque, Metro Manila offers many valuable insights.

According to its brief history, the San Dionisio Credit Cooperative was organized in 1961 with only 28 members and a cash position of P380. But early on, its chartered members had internalized the need for a new and long-term approach to community development that would make use of the indigenous resources of the people. They were looking for something more than a waiting shed and other standard donations. They were not happy with the traditional way of helping the community. They wanted the community to be able to stand on its feet. And they were encouraged in their goal by a strong faith in the potentials of the community. The reflection was clear, simple and incisive. Action was the natural consequence.

The first order of business was to organize a community body. The founding fathers of the San Dionisio Credit Cooperative were fortunate to have as their mentor Fr. Hogan, S.J., an acknowledged authority on the dynamics of social organizations. They were taught the principles and the techniques of building a community organization. But even before the learning process began, San Dionisio's initiators had already been equipped with the values and the mindset of successful organizers. They had shared experiences in their interface as Rover Scouts and as members of the Christian Family Movement. In short, their organizational start-up phase was not a *tabula rasa* but the application of deeply held ideals imbibed in scouting and Christian fellowship. Ideals such as *honesty, brotherhood, self-reliance, trustworthiness,* and *perseverance,* among others have become the operating article of faith.

Understandably, San Dionisio went through birth pains. The organizers had their ample share of ridicule from the fencesitters. There were community practices and outlook that had to be changed. There were power blocs that would be threatened. The possibility of the organizers' enthusiasm waning was another factor to consider. Plus the infectious doubt that perhaps the dream was too much for fallible mortals to give life to.

Now 29 years after, the San Dionisio Credit Cooperative has a roster of over 6,000 adult members with another 6,000 more (the children of adult members) enjoying associate membership status. Present asset level stands at over P40 million. By any standard, San Dionisio is a success story not only in cooperative development but also in people empowerment.

What are the ingredients of this success? As previously mentioned, the quality of leadership is a major driving force. San Dionisio could not have gone this far if its early builders and the second generation of leaders were not imbued with a missionary zeal. Running San Dionisio is not just a task. It is more of a mission.

Effective leadership at San Dionisio is complemented with responsive followership. The members of the cooperative from its very inception have been made to feel that they belong to the organization. Their dignity is respected. Their *palabra de honor* is presumed and recognized. An actual case is illustrative. A member-borrower who defaulted on his regular amortization was not treated as a delinquent account the way banks would react. The cooperative inquired as to the reason behind the default. The member-borrower was not "confronted" but approached so that he might avail of additional assistance from the cooperative. An additional accommodation was extended and the previous loan was restructured. Thus, the member concerned was saved the occasion of losing face. His sense of self-respect was reinforced.

To this member and to many others, the San Dionisio Credit Cooperative has *pagmamalasakit*. Little wonder then that they are committed to make it grow.

BEYOND CORPORATE WALLS

HUMANITIES FOR MANAGEMENT

THERE are practitioners of management who consider the field as a science with its own principles and methodologies. Others claim and teach that management is an application of mathematics or engineering. Mathematical models have been designed to approximate the functional relationships of key variables which affect the outcome of a managerial decision.

The reduction of management to a process of quantification is not difficult to understand. If management is to be measured in terms of its expected output, then every factor which directly contributes to the attainment of the final outcome has to be carefully calibrated. Nothing, as much as possible, should ever be left to chance. This was demonstrated during World War II by the United States in the management of the war efforts. Behind the victories achieved in Europe and the Pacific was the methodical marshalling of human forces, the effective maximization of physical resources, the training of military personnel, the timely production and distribution of material, the accuracy of intelligence data gathering activities, and the synchronization of all the nuts and bolts of the huge American war machine, among others.

In war as in peace, performance and results become overriding concerns. Hence the need for that discipline that *gets things done*. And if management precisely is the process of getting things done, then what the competitive world needs most are managers and their tools for producing results. *Efficiency* and *effectiveness* become the battlecry of a new breed of action specialists.

Little wonder then that postwar Europe perceived in the irrefutable successes of management science the "American Challenge." While the Old World gave birth to the Graeco-Roman civilization, the New World is the cradle of a new mindset that clearly defines objectives and zeroes in on specific approaches for attaining them. From the management centers of the United States has come out a new bibliography of efficiency-oriented technologies such as PERT/CPM, information systems, trend forecasting instruments, potential problem analysis tools, training laboratories, etc.

Understandably, this concern for results and for producing them has made management a distinctly practical discipline. A necessary by-product of such an outlook is the institutionalization of structures and systems, the formulation of strategies and the acquisition and transmission of skills all calculated to maximize productivity and to improve the bottomline.

Given such an organizational environment, every moment has to be productive. Every available space must contribute to overall efficiency. Every act has a measurable positive or negative value based on its conformity to prescribed standards.

Somewhere along the way, an organization so shaped develops reflexes that betray its human origin. In the name of pragmatism, and in pursuit of results, everything is permissible other than those expressly prohibited by law. People can be dismissed due to cost reduction measures. Human relationships established over the years in the corporate world can be terminated because of reorganization. The friendships, the fabric of trust intricately woven by the human components of an organization, the many intangible bricks of talents and commitment contributed by not a few in building an organization—all these can be set aside, as in fact they have been negated in some cases, precisely because they defy calculation. They have no cash value in a results-oriented culture. They are matters of sentiments which are intangible in a corporate world dominated by computer programmers, systems analysts, finance specialists, strategists, issues managers, apologists, market monitors, etc. They are perceived as standing in the way of change and growth.

No one may begrudge management for emphasizing quantification and analytical skills and for showing a bias for specialists. But to create a new culture based on results maximization to the exclusion of other equally relevant human concerns may have its own tradeoffs. By all means, people can look at the trees. But would it not be better if they can also see the forest? The managerial skills of planning, organizing, directing and controlling are necessary. And so is a wholistic perspective that goes beyond the *how's* into the ultimate *why?*

Which brings us to the relevance of the humanities for management. Philosophy, literature and the arts may not have a direct and immediate impact on productivity and the profit picture. In themselves they do not have any cash value. Philosophy cannot bake bread. Literature cannot increase the GNP. A work of Picasso or a creation of Bach cannot save a company in the process of liquidation. And yet they are desired in themselves because by their very nature they uplift the human spirit, open the mind to a world of infinite possibilities, and make the heart sensitive to the beauty and unity in the universe.

A manager who is acquainted with philosophy cannot fail to notice the greatness of the human mind as it is manifested in the ideas of Confucius, Plato, Aristotle, Aquinas, Locke, Descartes, Kant, Hegel, Whitehead, Russell, Wittgenstein, Buber, Marcel, Sartre, etc. The sense of intellectual humility that philosophy inspires in its student would be a desirable virtue for any manager. Management that lacks the humility to admit its limitations can be very destructive. It can be inhuman.

From the pages of literary masterpieces, a manager can gain precious insights into the complex human nature and the universal mainspring of human motivation. Shakespeare's works are like a comprehensive map of the full range of human emotions and how they are formed. The mystical writings of St. John of the Cross echo man's quest for God. The characters of Dostoevsky affirm that there is something fundamentally sacred about life. The poetry of Tagore transports the reader to an intimate communion with a caring nature. The novels of Rizal are timeless in their accurate portrayal of the cancerous cells that weaken society.

The great paintings, the classical music of the masters, the sculptural treasures, the architectural wonders and all the signatures of man's artistic sensitivity are one in giving witness to man's creative nature, to man's endless striving to add more to what nature has to offer. Nobody beholds a great work of art without being ennobled in the process.

Humanities heighten one's sensitivity to the things that eyes cannot see. They bring a manager face to face with what is really essential. They give meaning, coherence and purpose to a rapidly changing world. They find eternity in time, they discern the shape of a cathedral from an ordinary stone. And they sustain the restless striving for things that never were.

Humanities give management a reason for being.

CORPORATE DEMOCRACY

THERE is a season for distributing corporate annual reports as prepared by in-house PR departments with the professional help at times of creative design studios. Stockholders are invited to an annual meeting to hear a full accounting of stewardship from their board of directors and the management team.

No other event in the life of a corporation underscores the accountability of corporate stewards to the firm's owners more than the stockholders' meeting. The day itself is characterized by corporate legalese. A standard ritual has been prescribed which tends to reinforce the authority of stockholders over the board. The owners have the right to call the shots even for just a day. They can censure management. They can remove one, some, or all the members of the board.

To a large extent, the stockholders of a corporation may be compared to the citizens of a nation. Final authority rests in them. In short, *corporate sovereignty* belongs exclusively to them.

Indeed, there is a democratic framework within a corporation. A number of principles may be deduced from this. First, those tasked to be in charge of a company's operations are morally bound to live up to the stockholders' trust. They owe it to the owners to give them a fair return on their investments by maximizing profitability without necessarily sacrificing the other accountabilities to the employees, the customers, the suppliers and creditors, the immediate community, and the government. This requires a judicious use of limited resources, acute sensitivity to new market opportunities, continuous improvement of products and services, a productivity-oriented work ethic among employees, and a corporate environment where both the managers and the managed work willingly as a team.

Second, a stockholder should have access to corporate records of transactions entered into by management including information on other management decisions. This right of information is implicit in the right of ownership. If corporate democracy has to be meaningful, transparency is a must.

Third, the matter of management compensation must be evaluated from the standpoint of stockholders to insure that the rewards package does not unduly diminish what is due stockholders. Whether the system is fair and equitable must be viewed in the context of the prevailing industry practice, the interests of stockholders, and the profit performance record of management.

As the process of broadening the ownership base of corporations gains momentum, corporate managers will be confronted more and more with the growing voice of people who are aware and assertive of their rights as stockholders.

The manager who knows the workings of the new corporate democracy, its expectations and challenges and is prepared to respond to them creatively will likely succeed in the altered corporate environment.

PR IN A CHANGING MILIEU

THE *third wave* of Toffler or the *age of discontinuity* of Drucker has affected human society in general and compelled a change in the assumptions of many professions including Public Relations.

Both Toffler and Drucker call the attention of modern man to a convergence of events and forces that stress the vision of a common world. The quantum leap in information technology which has been largely made possible by a number of breakthroughs in the field of electronics and computer applications has altered man's perception of time and space. Time is now reckoned in terms of immediacy. Such terms as instant playback and feedback, fast track, and high speed processing underscore time's compression into the here and now. Space perception is no longer equated with static distances. The wonders of global satellite communication make any point on the planet just a phone call away. With direct dialing, Paris is just a few seconds away from Manila. Using teleconferencing technology, heads of state can have their own summit in living color without having to leave their respective offices.

We do not know for sure the precise directions of all these

developments. But this much is certain—the trends are discernible. Man's social environment is changing. Human values and expectations are being transformed. How then can the world of Public Relations remain the same?

Because the production and dissemination of new knowledge is happening at such a rapid pace, even attitudes and values of persons and institutions may change. When television goes to the countryside of a developing or underdeveloped country, the rural viewers are not just in contact with a new information medium but are brought closer to the world at large. Electronic journalism brings the events in Geneva or South Africa direct to the barrio via Domsat. At some point in time, both the content and level of awareness of people will expand.

The information explosion which characterizes the second half of the present century implies increase in knowledge. This suggests that those whose professional interests call for a lot of interaction with various sectors of society must recognize the presence of a knowledgeable public whose horizons keep on growing. Nothing hurts a profession more than an attitude of condescension. And this is even more so for Public Relations.

As a communicating and goodwill-seeking activity, Public Relations cannot afford to ignore the emerging issues and concerns which a changing environment creates. Also, it must know the shifts in public moods, sentiments and behavior. This means that the PR specialist must have a mechanism for keeping track with the fluctuations in public pulse.

An application of PR sensitivity to environmental factors shows that there is a climate of protectionism prevailing in the trading policies now of the US and the EEC. What is the underlying cause? What is ASEAN's strategy for coping with the problem? Will this elicit some form of hostility in ASEAN either collective or individual to any American or European MNC operating in the region?

Which brings us to the issue of doing PR or any other business activity in a cross-cultural context. Admittedly, there are universal principles for conducting business internationally or else international trade is impossible. An international medium of exchange, worldwide banking practices, and general agreements on tariffs, freights, and consular policies all facilitate the conduct of business among nations. But it must also be emphasized that international business is not just a matter of exchanging currencies, of buying and selling commodities, of applying internationally accepted principles of management. Business necessarily involves people. And people are products of a given culture.

If the people of a host country show some form of hostility to a Western MNC in its midst, it can be for a number of reasons. It can be due to the imposition of a spartan work ethic on native labor or to the overbearing posture of the expatriate executive. Whatever, there is a failure to understand the local culture and the sensibilities of the people. The mere fact that a host developing country badly needs foreign investments is no reason to gloss over what the local culture implies. And no amount of press releases, and not even the most impressive annual report can correct the damage arising from corporate ignorance of the values of the host country.

As world trade improves especially between ASEAN and EEC, between the Asia-Pacific countries and the US and Canada, there will be intensified MNC operations in the region with all the attendant cross-cultural encounter problems. MNCs can learn from the experiences of past and present religious missionaries, the Peace Corps, and diplomats. The challenge is clear—MNCs must look for expatriates who are not only good at getting things done but equally competent at managing people of a different culture.

Public Relations in a cross-cultural context requires different perspectives and skills. It calls for something of a global orientation, a desire to learn the language, the tradition, the anxieties, and aspirations of a strange milieu. It demands nothing less than trying to see the world through native eyes.

There are new realities to consider in the conduct of Public Relations in a fast changing world. Whereas before messages were easy to formulate and target publics readily identifiable, now the composition of a message depends on so many factors such as how it is affected by the larger situation, the credibility of the sender, the suitability of the channel or medium, the presence of barriers to communication, the need for feedback and evaluation. Public Relations has long ceased to be purely a public information job or a press relations work. For today the PR professional as a deserving member of the management team must address his competence to analyzing and interpreting the corporate environment, to studying social, political, and economic trends insofar as they have a bearing on the organization's philosophy, structure, strategy, people, and systems. To be able to do this, the PR person must be more than a press agent, an image specialist, or a wordsmith. He must have an interdisciplinary perspective, and be a corporate man for all seasons.

A CLOSER LOOK AT IMAGE ENGINEERING

ONE of the terms coined by the wordsmiths of the American PR industry is *image engineering*. On its face, the term suggests an attempt to gain added mileage for PR and to project it as a scientific discipline quite removed from the level of gut feel.

Undoubtedly, PR has evolved from the days of Ivy Lee and from the simple objective of earning public goodwill for a person or institution. The technology has improved considerably. PR has been elevated to the status of a top management responsibility. And to maintain acceptance in corporate board rooms and executive suites, PR must satisfy a managerial need—*measurable results*. Hence, the semantic device of equating PR with image engineering.

Who can question the use of the word *engineering* if the intent is to emphasize such aspects of PR as planning and measurement of results? Indeed, no PR professional can ignore the need to plan, to scan the corporate environment, to audit the strengths as well as the weaknesses of his client or employer, to prepare a program of action complete with budget, manpower, responsibility centers, timetable and implementation mechanics. Such devices as a comprehensive task list, PERT/CPM, and trend analysis are tools familiar to engineers. In this sense, there is something of engineering in PR. Moreover, a considerable area of PR requires quantification. The extent of message exposure, the immediacy of public recall, and shifts in public perceptions are all measurable.

The question, therefore, is not in creating an analogy between PR and engineering. The problem is in presuming that a personal or institutional image can be *engineered*. Are the so-called *image engineers* saying that one's image can be so crafted that it can with some contrivances change from negative to positive, from low to high? Are they assuming that the shape and direction of a person's perception can be programmed such that at a precise point the intended effect necessarily follows?

It is possible to have a mix of PR elements in measured proportion, i.e., the intrinsic attributes of the PR client, message content and structure, frequency of exposure, application of standard tools, and knowledge of the public's profile, among others. But there is no assurance that the desired results will take place. There is no absolute certainty that the anticipated chemistry will materialize. The PR product can be rejected by its target public. A change in public attitudes and perceptions cannot be manipulated.

For all the technological sophistication of the image engineers, there seems to be something basic that may have been overlooked. Winning public understanding, acceptance, and support is not just a matter of technology. PR is not just a question of form, of media mileage, of cosmetics. It is a public recognition of a substantive performance. It is goodwill rightfully earned.

If the goodwill of the public has to be deserved, then there is a moral dimension in PR. The public is not merely a statistical aggregate that can be played with at will. Individual persons constitute a public. As philosophers proclaim, persons are essentially *subjects*, never *objects*. Hyprocrisies, half-truths, lies, and manipulations violate the subjectivity of persons. This must be the reason why Saul of Tarsus said to the Corinthians that eloquence without charity is no more than cymbals clashing, empty bells ringing.

There is something deeply disturbing about the implications of image engineering. The term suggests a condescending outlook which is too cerebral and unfeeling. One cannot help discerning traces of arrogance, the presence of a mindset that views human behavior in a purely mechanistic mode outside the broader context of a complex sociocultural setting.

Were not image engineers engaged by a deposed dictatorship to shore up whatever was left of its public image after the assassination of Benigno S. Aquino, Jr.?

In contrast, the massive outpouring of public sympathy for Senator Aquino's widow was spontaneous, authentic and completely beyond the parameters of any conceivable PR program. EDSA was not the handiwork of image engineers. It was the consciousness of a nation coming to terms with itself.

IS THERE A UNIVERSAL MANAGER?

THE development of *professional management* as underscored by the corporate world's need for such a service and the academe's offering of various management education programs seems to have created a kind of mystique about this most contemporary science and art. In fact, a French observer credits the application of management principles in American business and industry as the clue to the US dominance in the world economy in the postwar years. To Europe, the "American Challenge" was the American mastery of the management discipline.

Thus, the word *management* came to be clothed with a positive aura of its own. Something of a cult of management took shape with its own literature, ritual, language, hierarchy and all. A master's degree from the Harvard Business School or INSEAD in Fontainebleau, France is a universal badge of distinction, often a key to exclusive executive suites.

When a company is in bad shape and needs an infusion of vision and vitality, a typical prescription is to get a good top man to run the show. The underlying assumption is—that the level of corporate performance is a function of the quality of management.

A firm that lacks an internal management capability normally looks outside for the right talents with the help of executive search agencies. Ideally, such talents should be sourced internally both for organizational morale and career development purposes. But this approach takes time for it entails the existence of an ongoing management development program. Hence, the phenomenon of corporate "headhunting."

But what can the top manager really offer? What professional skills does he have? What kind of vision can he provide? What fresh insights can he share? What sort of leadership can the corporation's people look up to in him?

He may have been a celebrated success in other enterprises. But this is no assurance that he will replicate his good track record so far in new or future challenges. There is something unreal about the idea of a *manager for all seasons*. A universal manager who can theoretically fit in any venture in any sector or industry is too abstract to be tangible. He is just like the perfect soldier or the perfect gentleman. The person in the flesh is too finite for perfection.

There may be a universality in the appreciation of the classical management functions. Who can argue against the transferability of such management disciplines as planning, organizing, directing, controlling and evaluating? These activities are as essential to GM as they are to Toyota. They are as crucial to San Miguel as they are to Heineken. They are as operative in Hyundai as they are in Siemens.

To the extent that management is a science with its own set of laws and verification methods, to the extent it qualifies as a transnational activity. But management as practiced is more of an art. Management in action is shaped by the realities of a given time and of a particular place. It is culture-bound.

Thus, there is something uniquely American about the way Mr. Iacocca manages Chrysler. Similarly, there is something uniquely Japanese about the way Mr. Morita runs Sony. Chrysler and Sony may have parallel concerns. Both organizations may be driven by an identical passion for quality and excellence. But they are different organizational systems with their respective strategies, skills, shared values, and personalities.

Rare is the manager who can ably and comfortably cross cultural boundaries. Rarer still is the manager who can succeed in managing an organization which is completely alien to his own training and background. Perhaps the only historical figure who succeeded in managing an organization of a different culture was the late Gen. Douglas MacArthur, the "American Caesar" for Occupied Japan.

General MacArthur was uniquely equipped for his job as the military administrator of a defeated adversary. He had immersed himself in the study of the Oriental mind and of the Japanese psyche. He knew intimately the premises of Japan's history. He was keenly sensitive to the feelings of a vanquished people. He restored their pride. He respected and preserved the symbol of their nationhood. And he gave them a blueprint for a better future. He was magnanimous in victory. The rest is now history.

Could somebody else have accomplished as much?

QUESTIONS FROM THE FUTURE

WHERETO?

NOT too long ago, former Vice President Emmanuel Pelaez who is now our ambassador to the United States nearly lost his life when his car was ambushed near his residence. While in a hospital he asked the late General Karingal a very disturbing question: "What is happening to our country, General?"

With apprehension and confusion we ask the same question now: *"What is happening to the Philippines?"*

Today we are confronted with the most serious crisis ever in our history as a nation. An unprecedented debt burden is taxing our ability to survive. Think of the huge budgetary outlay, about 40 percent of the national budget, which must be set aside just to service our foreign debt. We only have 60 percent left for our basic expenditures. Translated into what the common *tao* understands, this means that the budgetary pie for salaries, additional facilities, improvements, and maintenance has shrunk considerably.

Compounding the debt burden is the pressure of a growing population with increasing nutritional, shelter, educational, livelihood, and health care needs. It is too easy to say that we must produce more, that we have to sell more. But the global market is not readily hospitable to many of our traditional agricultural products. And even our nontraditional exports must contend with the protectionist mood prevailing in the advanced economies.

Up to now we are still looking for the main engine of economic growth. Is it the small-scale enterprise? If so, is there a concerted effort to encourage genuine private initiative? Bureaucracy, sad to say, is still very much around to discourage the growth of entrepreneurial spirit.

For sheer lack of domestic capital, we are compelled to attract foreign investments. We offer incentives in terms of a tax moratorium and profit repatriation. But are we competitive as an investment destination? How do we compare with the investment climate in Taiwan, Singapore, Thailand, Malaysia, and Indonesia? Surely, the current state of labor unrest is sending negative signals to prospective investors.

We can have the best blueprint for economic recovery. But without political stability, no economic miracle is possible. The growing insurgency coupled with a fragmented military threatens the life of a newly restored democracy. The CPP/NPA is relentless in its armed struggle. Its regulars are all over Luzon, the Visayas, and Mindanao. The NPA regulars in Bicol demonstrated their ability to isolate the peninsula from the rest of Luzon by blasting off a number of bridges. This is not to doubt the ability of the AFP to fight the insurgents.

But while the NDF has launched its own propaganda offensive and has activated its satellite organizations in pursuit of clearly defined goals, there has been no adequate matching effort on the part of government. One gets the impression that it is only the AFP that is fighting insurgency. As we very well know, a purely military solution to the problem will never work.

Meanwhile, the present government has created so much democratic space. It has succeeded in getting a new Constitution ratified. It has revived the concept of separation of powers with an independent judiciary and a bicameral legislature.

In addition we have other basic political and social institutions in place that have over the years managed to help keep the nation together. We have a career civil service. Our educational system is the envy of other developing countries. The family tradition of solidarity, of closing ranks in times of difficulties remains. We have a legion of skilled manpower. Our managerial class is comparable to the best in the world. We have demonstrated to ourselves and to the world that we are capable of responding constructively to any challenge. However, we can and we must do more than what has already been achieved.

The next question is—*where do we go from here?* We have basked too long under the euphoria of the EDSA Revolution. Perhaps our fault lies in our tendency to look back repeatedly, unmindful of the many urgent tasks at hand and unwilling to consider a range of options for the future. Could it be that we as a people lack that sense of urgency, coherence, and purpose that has made other nations great?

As a nation, we have shared memories and experiences and

common aspirations. But we need to emphasize our commonalities and internalize our sense of oneness. As an old saying goes, *united we stand, divided we fall*.

Still, we live as a cluster of islands. We speak in so many voices. We work at cross purposes. We are painfully in search of that elusive unity amidst diversity.

What is it that we really want? If we can only be single-minded in pursuing a unified direction! If we can at least define our priorities and address ourselves to doing first things first! Unfortunately we do not have the luxury of time.

The time to get our act together is now. For time is not in our favor anymore. We have made too many costly mistakes already. We cannot afford to commit some more.

In essence, what is at stake is not just the survival of the present government or the preservation of democracy. Hanging in the balance is the integrity of the nation and the fate of generations yet unborn.

Government alone cannot do the monumental job of repairing a shattered nation. The people must help in picking up and putting the scattered pieces together.

But who are the people? Where are the people? Who will light the candles of hope and keep them burning?

THE SEARCH FOR NEW HEROES

IN the late 40s and the very early 50s Japan used to be a reference point in assessing the stage of Philippine development. Maybe the comparison then was somewhat misplaced considering that Japan had already reached world power status even before World War II.

However, what other countries could the Philippines compare herself to then? Not any of the states in French-Indochina which must still reckon with the French Foreign Legion. Not Thailand with its idyllic ambience. Not Indonesia with the Dutch still clinging to the vestiges of colonial rule. Not the British protectorate of Malaya which had yet to survive the threat of a communist insurgency. Not Taiwan which served as a sanctuary for the retreating forces of the Kuomintang. Not Hong Kong with its continuous flood of refugees from China. Not Singapore which initially doubted its own ability to stand alone. And not South Korea which was at war with its northern half.

Sometime back then at that point in history when Japan was vanquished and the rest of Southeast Asia was a wasteland, the Philippines stood out as the country most likely to succeed for many reasons. The political infrastructure was intact. The Commonwealth government steeped in constitutional democracy was ready for self-rule. The civil service was operative. The judiciary was working. The educational system was in place.

Somewhere in our journey to the future, our potentiality for getting *there* failed to materialize. The Philippines even this late is not yet within the circle of the "Tiger Economies." And even the recent comparative achievements of Thailand, Malaysia and Indonesia (let alone Singapore, Taiwan, South Korea and Hong Kong) vis-a-vis our own is an eye-opener indeed. Once more, we have been left out. We are not among the new NICs.

How can we ever explain that we who were once ahead in the region economically are now lagging behind? Assuming that our neighbors will simply stand still to wait for us, can we really catch up? And because they are moving forward with such a purposeful pace, what chances do we have of getting closer to where they are now?

It is too tempting to blame our misfortune on others. Others bewail the remaining structures of colonialism. Or the feudal character of Philippine society. Or the crippling burden of a huge foreign debt. Or the miseducation of the Filipino. Or the pains of the rebirth of democracy. Or the prevalence of divisive politics.

All these partly explain the structural dimension of our ills. But there are attitudinal factors as well which have been underscored by social scientists. Such psychosocial tendencies as *crab mentality, ningas-talahib, bahala na, bukas na, mahina ang loob,* and *kanya-kanya,* among other things, constitute a formidable phalanx of restraining forces that hinder the historical momentum towards progress. Hence, the emphasis on value formation as a strategic component of national development.

The danger, however, lies in looking at value formation as

something of an off-the-shelf solution to the pestering problem without realizing that the application of the prescription has a much wider time horizon. We do not form values overnight. Moreover, we do not just begin and end with the dissemination of cherished beliefs. They have to be accepted freely. They have to be deeply internalized. And having instilled them they have to be translated into specific acts and sustained repeatedly until a discernible positive character emerges.

In the communication of these values, the moral credibility of their articulators is most essential. At issue is no longer the eloquence of the disseminator but his being perceived as the embodiment of the things he believes in. In short, the whole process is not just a mental exercise. More, it is an effective experience of sharing hopes, insights and perspectives.

There are pedagogical implications involved in the formation of values. For instance, at the conceptual level, the mind of the intended receiver is not a *tabula rasa* on which the value disseminator may just impress certain ideals. If it were, then the whole process is just a matter of information flow. As every good teacher knows from experience, the mind of the student at any stage of its development has its own thought process, its unique way of perceiving and processing bits of sensory data. This is, more or less, what students of philosophy remember as the *categories of the mind* from their recollection of Kant.

The sensitivity of Oriental temper coupled with the predominantly affective side of the Spanish character must have molded the Filipino mind to look for things beyond the cerebral and the logical.

Thus, it is pointless to aim primarily at the cognitive side of the Filipino mind without at the same time addressing the heart or the *damdamin*. It is wishful thinking to hope for a change *of* the Filipino unless his *kalooban* is touched and transformed. And the inner self cannot be uplifted without its consent and active participation.

The dynamics of moral renewal calls for a person-oriented pedagogy of sincerity, consistency, humility, and hope. The value carrier, like any of the early apostles, must be an authentic witness to the truths he lives for. Only then can he be an effective catalyst in the collective reflection of a people he must deliver from despair.

When committed apostles come, can divine grace be far behind?

IN SEARCH OF THE CRITICAL MASS

MANY have bewailed the comparative disadvantage of the Philippines vis-a-vis its neighbors. For in many points of comparison, the nation suffers when seen in relation to South Korea, Singapore, Taiwan, Hong Kong and Thailand. But why?

How could a country that helped South Korea defend itself, that has more natural resources than what Singapore can ever dream of, that has more universities and professional managers than what Taiwan can offer, that has more English-speaking citizens than what Hong Kong has, and that trained the agricultural experts of Thailand—ever be far behind?

The wounded national pride was compelled to make a public statement that the next economic miracle in Asia shall be the Philippines. However, the question is—will the Philippines make it? Is there a national consensus to get rid of the stigma of being *kulelat?* Is there a collective will to aim high and to reach the goal? What does it take to get *there?*

First, there is need to take stock of national strengths, resources, capabilities as well as shortcomings. On the positive side, the Philippines has a rich historical legacy and a number of institutions to build a better future on. The 1896 Revolution, the first of its kind in Asia, demonstrated early on a national capacity for self-reliance. The proclamation of Philippine Independence in 1898 and the subsequent inauguration of the First Philippine Republic in 1899 which were both historic Asian milestones proved that Filipinos even then were already a highly developed political community with a keen sense of their own destiny. The Malolos Constitution of 1899 was a clear demonstration of the nation's political maturity.

Even with the American colonization of the Philippines, the process of institution building was not impaired. In fact, the United States introduced a number of sociopolitical systems such as a public education, a civil service and a framework of government, among others, which are still operational. That these American transplants developed roots on Philippine soil was proof enough of the recipient's natural adaptability, a factor much needed in any recovery program.

Not even the horrors of World War II succeeded in destroying the spirit of a young nation. From the ruins of 1945 emerged a collective will to move forward. In spite of the national anguish over the loss of countless loved ones and the destruction of thousands of homes, the nation went through the herculean task of picking up the shattered pieces of a simple past with which to start a new future. All the psychological elements of a successful rehabilitation were present. There was a shared experience of tragedy. There was courage. There was so much hope. There was no other way to go but up.

Thus, when independence was restored in 1946, the Philippines stood out among all the colonies that were about to regain their freedom. In the first place, the Philippines was very much unlike any of many African and Asian colonies. There were preexisting sociopolitical infrastructures to start with, i.e., schools in all levels, religious institutions, a legal system, a judicial machinery and a government bureaucracy. Natural resources were bountiful. Also, there were entrepreneurs, craftsmen, bankers, managers and industrialists. In short, all the ingredients that could make the Philippines the first NIC in Asia were available.

In addition, the Philippines as a peace-loving country and as the third largest English-speaking nation had access to a bigger world. Filipino students were learning new skills and technologies in American universities which could have practical applications for the country's development needs. Moreover, Japan had started to deliver on its moral obligations to the Philippines through the reparations payments. There was no foreign exchange rate problem to contend with. External debt was not yet a disturbing reality. Hardly did the people hear of budgetary deficits.

Of course there was already an insurgency problem. But it was localized only in Central Luzon and in a part of Panay. Moreover, the Huk rebellion was basically rural in operation and, therefore, seemed more tractable.

And yet in spite of the historical convergence of all the factors that could have made the Philippines the first Asian NIC, the desired chemistry did not materialize. The point of critical mass was never reached.

Admittedly, the postwar reconstruction efforts had triggered off a momentum that was sustained in varying degrees by all succeeding administrations after Roxas. But no successful take-off has ever been made. Worse, the runway now is not as well paved and as clear as it was before. There are hazardous mounds and holes.

What then is missing? What sort of catalyst is necessary that will ignite a chain reaction of sustained achievements which in turn will propel the nation to defy the gravity of its own failures? What is that elusive element or the configuration of elements that will push the nation to the threshold of the future?

Many reasons have been advanced to explain why up to now the nation remains grounded while its neighbors are already airborne, why and how things go wrong. For all her shortcomings, however, the Philippines has what it takes to get *there*. The nation is not wanting in the crucial achievement factor. There are enough living models of achievement, real achievers who show the way. These are institutions and individuals who dare go against the negative forces of defeatism, parochialism and timidity. Such pacesetters as San Miguel Corporation, United Laboratories, SGV, Mina Gabor of CITEM and Lilia Calderon-Clemente of the investment management community of New York, to mention some, may as well be the nucleus of a new nation of achievers.

When this nucleus reaches the point of critical mass, enough creative energy shall be unleashed for that much awaited blastoff.

BUILDING BLOCKS FOR TOMORROW

INSTITUTION BUILDING

THE revival of democracy in the Philippines is being accompanied with unnecessary birth pains.

Understandably, the birth of any complex being is part of the stressful process of growing. But to be born again, as it were, is to be free from reliving prior injuries. This is precisely what *renewal* means—to start fresh by building on the lessons of the past.

However, in the case of democracy's revival in the Philippines, the signs of renewal are blurred. What we see is not the phenomenon of rebirth. It is as if democracy is being tried as a political experiment for the very first time. It is as if there is no recollection of what democracy was like before.

Hence, all the start-up problems. But a rationalization of the shortcomings of today's democracy may induce a risky sense of normalcy. The troubles we perceive in the way the mechanisms of democracy are being operated are really deviations from people's expectations. Unless these perceptions are modified through tangible improvements in the current political system, the pains of birth may prove fatal.

A vision or an idea grows for a number of reasons. First, there is a true dreamer who believes in his cause to the point of self-sacrifice. Second, there are enough disciples equally committed to spread their master's gospel. Third, there are carpenters and masons skilled in building the architectural expression of a belief. Fourth, there are the maintenance people who attend to the day-to-day task of keeping the whole structure in good shape. All these are as true for a religious faith as they are for a political ideology.

In the case of Christianity, the article of faith has survived to this day because of painstaking institutionalization. The theology, the liturgy, the architecture, the recruitment and training of promoters and the other underpinnings of organizational continuity have all been institutionalized. Thus, the singers and the preachers may come and go. But the song remains. The essential message never disappears.

Can we then say that the song of democracy can survive its singer? Can the democratic ideal live long after its believer has faded from the scene? Hopefully. And yet hardly. For the institutions that ought to embody the spirit of democracy have yet to be strengthened. Right now, they are battered by the tempest of public criticism which, unless creatively tamed, can deteriorate to popular indignation.

Indeed, democracy as revived is too fragile because its institutional foundation has not yet been firmly anchored on the consciousness of the Filipino people. It is one thing to affirm the virtues of an idea. But giving it structural support is another.

What compounds the problem confronting democracy in the Philippines today is the ever growing pressure of people's expectations. Failure to deliver on these hopes necessarily invites frustrations which are a fertile ground for spawning the seeds of democracy's destruction.

It is of course very unfortunate that the institution which directly represents the voting population is suffering from an erosion in public esteem. The House of Representatives whose members are supposed to be the voices of their respective rural and urban constituencies is saddled with not just a serious image problem but more so with an impaired self-concept. The continuous barrage of print and broadcast media criticisms cannot fail to dent the self-confidence of even the brave.

Those who may still have sympathies for the House as collegial body can very well appeal for sobriety and understanding. Why should the perceived sins of one or some members affect the integrity of the entire institution? And why not?

Perhaps ordinary people who, after all, are the real sovereign in any true democracy look at political realities through the prism of their simple life. They look up to their elected representatives for the fulfillment of the promise at EDSA. Their folk wisdom can easily discern any sign of betrayal. There is no gray area in their perception. It is either black or white.

There is still time for institutional mending. But this would require the active participation and direct involvement of every member. For any chain is only as strong or as weak as the smallest link.

THE GOVERNMENT AS AN ORGANIZATION

MANY of the perceived inadequacies of government may be traced to its organizational structure. The hierarchy, the way functions are delineated, the degree of clarity by which duties and responsibilities are defined, the dynamics of relationships between and among operating units, and the many layers of decision centers— all these combine to determine both the quantity and quality of the entire government performance.

The structure of government as it is described in the present Constitution is *presidential*, i.e., the executive and legislative functions are lodged in separate and distinct branches of government. This structure, as any student of political science knows, is premised on the principle of separation of powers with its system of checks and balances.

That the people chose to go back to the presidential structure of government by ratifying the 1986 Constitution signalled a popular rejection of the brief experiment with something that looked like a parliamentary system. But perhaps the repudiation of the previous set up was not so much directed at the parliamentary structure itself as it was against the person who authored the experiment. Whether it was the person or his creation that was the object of rejection hardly matters now. The people have spoken. Enough with the excesses of one-man rule and the perils of a very powerful presidency.

With such a logic, the revival of the presidential system was a foregone conclusion. The doctrine of separation of powers was forcefully argued. And if there is now so much concern about the preservation of either the executive or the legislative turf, a major reason may be the strict application of the principle.

Separation of powers is essential to the survival of democracy. But for a new government of a developing country simultaneously confronted with too many problems on several fronts, there is an urgent need for workable mechanisms of coordination. Unfortunately, the return of the presidential system has not necessarily brought back the instruments of executive-legislative cooperation that were present in the pre-martial law administrations.

In the legislative branch for instance, the sheer physical distance that separates the Senate from the House of Representatives is a major hindrance to smooth interchamber interaction. Even with the conveniences of modern communications, there is no substitute to actual face-to-face meetings on a regular basis. Little wonder then that not a few observers think that either chamber feels alienated from the other. Add to this the fact that the Speaker of the House and the Senate president belong to separate political camps.

Between the executive branch and the legislature, there is actually little space devoted to collaborative work. Congress is too assertive of its power of the purse and its other constitutional prerogatives. And rightly so. Some members of the Cabinet are impatient about the pace of the legislative process. And they are right too. Contrasting perceptions, however, affect the delivery of basic services to a suffering nation.

What complicates the tug-of-war further is the unique situation whereby the head of the executive branch does not belong to any political party. In the past, the president's leadership of the party in power was a means for resolving differences with partymates in the legislature. Party caucuses attended by and often presided over by the president were effective vehicles for forging a common party stand on vital national issues.

Surely, the executive branch has a liaison officer assigned to each chamber of Congress. But these liaison officers, no matter how competent, fall outside the purview of the traditional political party machine. In this sense, their effectivity in bridging the gap between the two branches of government is very much limited.

From all indications, the government is a suitable candidate for **Organizational Development.**

LOYALTY TO THE CONSTITUTION

LOYALTY to the constitution is an ideal highly desired in any state that has its own popularly ratified fundamental law. For such an adherence, be it individual or collective, to a body of beliefs, values and aspirations provides continuity and stability in a political community.

Such loyalty to a set of principles on which the ultimate validity of any act of government rests is best exemplified and readily perceived in countries with a strong tradition of constitutionalism. The United Kingdom and the United States are famous examples. The British do not have a formally written constitution. And yet the British attachment to the ideals of the rule of law, free speech, and the supremacy of the people is legendary. The Americans are not far behind. Their commitment to the spirit of the US Constitution is almost religious in its intensity.

It can be said that both the British and the Americans "live" their respective constitutions. In both cases, there has been a deep and solid internalization of the fundamental truths enshrined in the constitution. This development has had a time scale spanning more than 200 years. Little wonder then that what their respective constitutions stand for are indelibly etched in the minds and hearts of the British and the Americans.

In such situations, the constitution ceases to be a mere piece of paper or a verbalization of certain thoughts. The constitution is thus transformed into something like the people's article of faith which gets "incarnated" in their perspectives and deeds. The constitution then becomes a living and authentic covenant, a sacred vessel that contains the distillation of the yearnings of all generations past and present. That kind of constitution is what people live and are prepared to die for.

When the message of the constitution begins to live in the consciousness of a people and to find nourishment in the continuing pursuit of a collective vision, no force on earth is destructive enough to erase it. But when the constitution for all its skillfully crafted phraseology is made a tool of convenience to be invoked to justify an act or to be overlooked when it is politically expedient, then it is desecrated to the level of meaningless words, of "empty bells ringing, cymbals clashing."

This desecration of the constitution was the hallmark of the rejected dictatorship. The 14 years of the dictatorship had deprived the Filipino people of a fundamental law they could authentically call their own. Whether or not the dictator's imposed constitution was truly ratified by the people is no longer an issue. In all the years of manipulations and deceptions, the people somehow could not care less if there was a constitution or not. It was as if the mind of the people was programmed to be indifferent to "constitutional" issues. Why bother? The word of the dictator was the law.

Surely, we now have a new constitution that has a stamp of the people's approval. But sad to say, it is at this point no more and no less than a comprehensive statement of political principles and ideals. Call it the most vital legal testament of the entire nation. But unless its lofty thoughts are translated into tangible acts that ordinary folks can easily perceive, it remains a mere piece of paper of interest only to teachers and students of political law.

Which brings us to a disturbing question: how can there be loyalty to something inanimate, to something that is not within the day-to-day experiences of many Filipinos? Is it not too much to expect people to give allegiance to a body of affirmations that are still so new as to have the smell of printer's ink in them? How can there be personal commitment to an abstraction? How can the farmer, the fisherman, the teacher, the student, the police officer, the soldier or anybody for that matter pledge to defend the constitution that has not been the subject of a nationwide multisectoral reflection?

One can recite a prescribed oath of allegiance to the flag or the constitution. But unless the person fully understands and deeply feels what each word means and requires, the articulation is only a symbolic act. What is needed is to experience with the heart the substance behind the form, the reality behind the gesture.

DEMOCRACY'S REASON FOR BEING

A top official of an ASEAN country once talked about the failures of democracy in the Philippines.

The observer did not look kindly at the effects of the democratic process restored by EDSA. Press freedom was criticized for its excesses. The system of checks and balances was questioned for its tendency to dissipate time and energy.

These outsider's perceptions of the workings of our own political systems can draw pointed rebuttals from those intimately familiar with and sympathetic to the meanderings of Philippine democracy. What is more important is to see the logic behind the criticism. The anti-democracy bias is premised on the assumption that the full exercise of freedom is intrinsically inimical to the progress of a developing country.

Others say that democracy works best in advanced economies and older political societies. Hence, the American and the British democratic systems. As the argument goes, democracy has succeeded in the United States and the United Kingdom because it has been there long enough to develop firm roots. A racist position tries to see a correlation between the mechanisms of democracy and the temper of Anglo-Saxons. A Western orientation cannot seem to imagine democracy thriving outside its Graeco-Roman moorings.

Democracy, admittedly, is culture-bound. Which means that a particular democracy as it has evolved somewhere cannot be transplanted elsewhere to replicate itself completely. A transplant can be rejected. But it can also be accepted even with modification.

For all the differences among various democratic models, there are essential commonalities present. Foremost among the least common denominators of all democracies is the recognition of the supremacy of the people as manifested through periodic popular elections. Implicit in this is respect for people's wisdom. Another common thread running through the fabric of democratic societies is the guaranty of the exercise of basic human rights.

Those who are too impatient in getting things done in the name of national development can become uneasy about the democratic process. Consultations with the people are time consuming.

Moreover, visionaries who are driven by a visionary zeal feel that they know what is good for the people. The next step is for them to start sounding as if they really speak for the people.

This condescending attitude is common to all dictators. The dictator, so he claims, knows best. He promises to deliver the people to a better future. An impoverished society out of survival may prefer bread to freedom. There is no dictator who believes that bread and freedom can be both enjoyed at the same time.

As a tradeoff, the promise of economic prosperity may be substituted for the enjoyment of democracy. This was the basic premises of Mr. Marcos when he imposed martial rule on a freedom-loving people. For a very brief period the promised blessings were almost there. A national ideology was crafted and imposed. Slogans were contrived. Discipline was prescribed. The propaganda machine tried to project the dictator as a benevolent ruler who would liberate the nation from poverty. Meanwhile, the people were totally left out in the making of decisions that affected their future. The destiny of present and future generations was mortgaged in secrecy. And the controlled media could not even dare make a whimper of protest.

What was tragic about this experiment in one-man rule was the deep wound it had inflicted on the Filipino psyche. The nation was reduced to a state of docility, to a sense of resignation, to an accommodation with the specious proposition that the ruler was indispensable. For who would dare defy the apparatus of dictatorship? And even if one or two or a few were bold enough like Don Quijote to fight the windmills, what were the chances of making it to the stars instead of hitting dirt and mud?

The experiment, however, was doomed to fail. The Filipino people could not contain their moral outrage. They found the courage to redeem their freedom. The shots at the tarmac marked the beginning of the end of the dictatorship. The national grief over the death of the man who eloquently said—"The Filipino is worth dying for!"—gave birth to a new nation committed to bring democracy back.

If the roots of democracy had not sunk deep in the hearts of Filipinos, there would not have been any EDSA Revolution to speak of. Thus, EDSA was not the handiwork of some personalities alone. It was the rebirth of a democratic nation.

And so democracy is back as a tool for charting the future of more than 60 million people based on a shared history and common aspirations. It is not a perfect system. But in spite of its shortcomings, its noise, confusion and all, it has balancing virtues. The air of freedom which the democratic space generates and radiates can be abused. But the same atmosphere breeds spontaneity and creativity not present in a repressed society. Where ideas are allowed to compete, something that is universally beneficial always comes out. The spirit of tolerance that inspires democracy is even reassuring to the less endowed.

Democracy is self-cleansing and self-rejuvenating. But to make it an effective instrument of national development, its leadership must have a transformative vision so that the people may be moved to seek wider horizons as they begin to actualize their vast potentials. A corollary gift is the ability to orchestrate various sectors to rise above narrow interests so that the end result will be a splendid national performance.

Freedom is not enough. It needs purpose and direction.

TOWARDS GREATER PRODUCTIVITY

THE Philippines today is saddled with a huge economic burden. Consequently, the need to surmount the crisis has never been more urgent, eliciting a number of prescriptions to achieve economic recovery.

Some economists offer such macro structural solutions as debt rescheduling, new credit availments, tight control of the money supply, additional tax measures, drastic cuts in public expenditures, and aggressive export promotions, among others. But what seems overlooked in the frenzied search for workable alternatives is the micro component, i.e., the human factor and its productivity that can and ought to make recovery realizable.

Productivity, however, as a concept is not value-neutral. It does not mean one and the same thing to all sectors. To workers used to industrial disputes, productivity may mean more hours of work, less leisure and more profit for stockholders. To a highly task-oriented management, the term may be equated with work simplification and time maximization. To economic planners, productivity is related to greater purchasing power which stimulates effective demand, higher employment and greater output.

Using the output-input ratio as a point of reference, productivity can be enhanced under any of the following possibilities: 1) output is constant but with a decreased input; 2) output is increased using the same amount of input; and 3) output and input are increased but the latter's share is less. Improving productivity in any of these situations entails better utilization of available resources and facilities.

Since the state of industrial peace is fairly indicative of the level of productivity in a given society, it would be useful to focus on the realities of the relationship between labor and management in the Philippines. The ideal of industrial peace has yet to become a continuing reality. Various laws have been enacted in pursuit of this objective. But one begins to wonder if industrial peace can be legislated. The written law defines only what can be done, what is prohibited, and what is obligatory. Legal and judicial institutions are supposed to insure that rights are respected and duties fulfilled. But the dynamics of harmonizing rights and duties is an entirely different human undertaking outside the fixed provisions of the law.

Industrial peace is a state of mind, a basic outlook that feeds on certain cultural roots, an aspiration validated by events in the history of a nation. It cannot be mandated anymore than war can be outlawed. It is unfortunate though that Philippine labor-management relations have taken an adversarial character. This need not have been so considering that there are elements in the Filipino culture supportive of a workable collaborative model. Thus within the nation's value system, there are conflict- reducing and consensus-building traits such as *puedeng kausapin* (openness to dialogue), *marunong magmalasakit* (capacity for empathy), *marunong makisama* (readiness to cooperate), *may hiya* (sense of self-respect), *marunong tumanaw ng utang na loob* (capacity for gratitude), and *mapagbigay* (conciliatory), to mention some. If these traits have not effectively influenced the direction of labor-management relations in the country, one reason could very well be the unquestioning adoption of a Western mechanism, i.e., collective bargaining as the fulcrum for resolving industrial disputes.

Historically, collective bargaining as a social process has been confrontational in nature. It operates on the assumption that labor has rights it must assert and defend and that management has basic prerogatives it should uphold. In its early beginning, the institution of collective bargaining in American industries was required by the prevailing social environment. Labor must organize to fight for its interests against the excesses of capital. But the inherent class conflict in the early days of the American capitalist economy did not evolve into a class struggle witnessed in socialist countries. Rather, the conflict was kept as much as possible within the confines of the collective bargaining process. In time, the mechanism developed its distinct culture and its own ritual.

To appreciate the confrontational spirit of the collective bargaining process as it evolved in the United States and as it subsequently moved to the Philippines, it would be pertinent to mention two factors: 1) the influence of a mechanistic theory of management popularized by Frederick Taylor; and 2) labor's apprehension that it was not getting a fair return for its contribution. Taylor's "scientific management" places too much emphasis on efficiency, time savings and work measurement. Out of Taylor's legacy came what is often referred to as *industrial engineering,* a term with much wider applications than Taylor's original system.

During Taylor's time (1856-1917), so much controversy had been generated by the "scientific management" theory. When efficiency becomes a fixation in any management theory and practice, workers stand the risk of being perceived largely in terms of their functions. Then a set of assumptions about people, one of which is "Theory X" as discussed by Douglas McGregor, would have to follow if only to give the practice a measure of logical validity.

Expectedly, the school of thought initiated by Taylor would be criticized for being too cerebral and unfeeling, and for its dehumanizing effects. In fact, the whole existential literature on man's alienation in an industrial society can be addressed to the teachers and practitioners of "scientific management." But the initial objection failed to dampen American industry's enthusiasm for Taylor.

"Scientific management" was contemporaneous to the early stage of America's colonial thrust into the Pacific. And as McKinley's expansionist vision took hold of the American psyche, the wheels of industry must be well-oiled and all engines revved up at full speed. There was no room for inefficiency.

A mechanistic interpretation of industrial relations could only elicit workers' perception that management is manipulative. That perception which has traces of class consciousness persists even today. One has only to recall the encyclical *Rerum Novarum* (1891) of Pope Leo XIII to see the dark side of industrialization. The emergence of the labor union as a social institution could not be dissociated from the need of workers to defend themselves against the abuses of a purely capitalist economy. Workers must organize to fight for their rights and to get their just share in the fruits of their toils.

As the United States established political and economic supremacy in the Philippines, America's model for promoting industrial peace was adopted in the colony. With the benefit of hindsight, it should have been discernible even at its inception that collective bargaining is only a tool for bringing together two subsectors of an organization to resolve underlying disputes. But it does not remove the polarization. In fact the process itself underscores the need to protect a sector's turf by utilizing to the hilt all available negotiating skills.

Underneath the present framework of industrial relations in the Philippines is labor's resentment of management and the latter's perception that workers only care about wage increases and additional fringe benefits. Evidently there is a wide communication gap. No less than the current state of labor unrest attests to this. Bridging this gap is necessary not only for the sake of industrial peace but as a precondition for productivity.

Perhaps the management community should make a self-appraisal of its own philosophy insofar as it has a bearing on labor-management relations. Are there no alienating elements in the management culture? It is just possible that the Filipino manager's management training which has a distinct American influence may have imparted such task-oriented skills as planning, budgeting, controlling, financial analysis, marketing research, etc. without a commensurate learning experience in the sociocultural disciplines. Business management schools that put a heavy stress on quantitative subjects may unwittingly convey the message that management's main job is to maximize profits and to get the job done in the most efficient way possible. Once the message sinks in, it is translated into attitudes and actions which all combine to create the impression that management is primarily interested only with money. Nothing can hurt the sensitive Filipino worker more.

The present economic crisis may yet be the triggering factor for bringing labor and management together to recast the foundation of their relationship. Change is in order. One may look at the process from either side of an organization. But to be a constructive participant, one should have the humility to accept that he could be a cause of the problem and the vision to think that he could also be a solution. Thus, management on its own initiative may try to reflect on its own philosophy, strategies, practices, training, systems, style, and culture. What is there in its words, deeds, and gestures that tends to alienate the workers? Is it so task-oriented as to ignore the human side of the enterprise? Does it inspire confidence in its decisions? Does it see the person in the worker? Does it lead by example? Does it have the compassion to understand human frailties? Is it sensitive to the subtle forces that stimulate the mind and uplift the heart of the Filipino?

A new self-awareness on the part of management is just the beginning of that long process of improving the climate for labor-management relations. There is also a need for an objective assessment of the psychological climate that pervades in the whole organization. Such a diagnostic work using a mix of research tools can indicate the level of organizational maturity, the degree of trust, the barriers to communication, the sense of commitment to organizational objectives, the values and expectations of the work force, labor's perceptions of management, the forces that make change possible, and the likely change agents.

There will be roadblocks along the way as management tries to initiate organizational change. Good intentions are not enough. Messages do not get accepted just because they are well composed and sincerely given. Having been accustomed to a confrontational mode of interaction, people will put meaning in words and believe what they want to believe. With more reason, therefore, that management should attempt to get out of the CBA syndrome. The same holds true also for labor. It takes only one to put up a wall. But it requires more than one to build a bridge.

If labor and management are willing to explore any viable approach to improve their relationship, then an intervention may be tried through the facilitation of an external organizational development specialist who is knowledgeable about the dynamics of social change. There can be a union-management intergroup dialogue which has nothing to do with the CBA. Briefly, the process calls for the selection by both labor and management of their key representatives to the intergroup session. Ideally, the whole exercise is conducted in a neutral venue which can be in any out-of-town location.

The initial session starts with an orientation during which the external facilitator explains the objectives of the process, his own expectations, and what the participants may expect in return. Then each participant may express his thoughts and feelings on how he sees himself in relation to the exercise. In short, something of a psychological contract is established at the start. The main focus is for labor and management through their representatives to develop images of themselves and their impressions of each other. These images are then exchanged across the two groups for clarification. What follows after is a group diagnosis of the present labor-management relationship. Assessments are subsequently exchanged. Finally there is a clarification of the key sources of friction.

This particular intervention is useful for the insights it provides. It enables both labor and management to be aware of the blind spots in their respective self-images, to stand as it were before a mirror to see their reflections. The atmosphere may still carry some traces of confrontation but because the learning exercise is not at all concerned with the CBA, there are enough reasons for it to be less adversarial.

New perspectives learned from this dialogical encounter may now be used as building blocks for future meetings where the problems of the industry, the state of the firm, and the economic needs of workers are discussed with candor but hopefully in a less hostile situation. As the organizational climate improves, as the people in an enterprise learn to focus more on the things they have in common, the time has come for labor and management to address a joint concern—working together to attain greater productivity.

A NEW BEGINNING

BRIGHT NOTES

LATEST available World Bank figures on the comparative agricultural performances of some countries in ASEAN show that the Philippines is doing fairly well in relation to its neighbors. In terms of per capita income in agriculture, the Philippines had posted from 1965 to 1985 a growth rate of 3.4% compared to Thailand's 1.2% and Indonesia's 1.9%.

These statistical data indicate that the Philippines which is basically an agricultural country is not at the tailend when it comes to a major sphere of its national concerns. For a true measure of a nation's capacity for achievement is precisely in an area where by tradition and by natural endowments it is supposed to do well. Agriculture is that area.

Actually, the country has what it takes to prosper agriculturally. It has a good natural resource profile. It has the rural manpower. It has an institutional infrastructure exemplified by no less than the leading agricultural training center in the region. And it has a corps of agri-technicians with tangible presence in every municipality of each province.

In addition, the principal agency mandated to oversee agriculture has a clear-cut vision and a specific mission statement which are both designed to usher in a higher level of agricultural achievements.

The pursuit of greater heights, however, requires new pathways and an appreciation of time and other constraints. Agriculture cannot really move faster forward without taking into account the promises offered by relating itself to industrial development. The immediate question then is—how to effect a synergistic blending of the growth requirements of both the rural and urban sectors.

Another area of serious concern is the rate of demographic expansion which outpaces the actual performance of agriculture. In short, the increase in productivity is not sufficient to cope with population pressure. What makes the whole situation even more challenging is the reduction of the total hectarage available for agriculture. Implicitly, the urgency of maximizing output cannot be overemphasized.

Government cannot be all things to all. And yet it is expected to address every front, to provide an answer to every problem, to be practically everywhere. One necessarily gets the feeling that the whole public bureaucracy is overextending itself in its desire to do much more.

To the great majority of Filipinos—the small farmers and fishermen whose sense of hard work is of public knowledge, government serves well by being a catalyst of agri-based entrepreneurial activities. In fact, quite a number of small agri-entrepreneurs in Luzon, Visayas and Mindanao are helping to provide new directions for Philippine agriculture through their initiative, self-help, resourcefulness and daring. This is a process that has already started without much fanfare. Ripples have been made. In time, the momentum if sustained well enough will create unstoppable waves.

Here is one scenario of development that offers so much hope to a nation in crisis.

A REASON FOR HOPE

THE birth anniversary of the late President Manuel L. Quezon is perhaps the right occasion for us to reflect on how far we have gone in our journey to nationhood, how faithful we have been to the ideals of the great leader, and how close we are to the dream of those who came before us.

These questions for reflection are necessary if we must plan for the future. Before we decide on where we want to go, we must first review the early steps we made, recall how we got to where we are now, and then find out what does it take or what else do we need to get to a desired destination.

We use Quezon as a point of reference for many reasons. It was he who provided the proper beginning for our national development. His sense of patriotism was the moving spirit of his generation. His crusade for Philippine independence was a lifetime obsession. His vision of an indivisible nation set into motion the transformation of a cluster of islands into a community of Filipinos sharing a common history and dreaming of a common future.

In Quezon's time there was the making of a great nation. Unfortunately, many years after, the process has been stalled. Right now, we stand the risk of slipping farther down the roster of developing countries in Asia. Thailand, Malaysia and Indonesia are already ahead. Meanwhile, Vietnam is catching up. We do not have much time left because we have wasted a large part of it.

Even as we must hold the nation together, we are confronted with formidable forces that seek to dismember us. From the left, the insurgents have not given up the armed struggle. They may still be far from achieving strategic victory but they continue to pose a serious threat to political stability. And from the right, military adventurism still causes public anxiety. The memory of failed coup attempts still lingers in people's mind.

Meanwhile, economic indicators do not show a rosy picture. Inflation keeps on eroding the value of the peso. The huge foreign debt is exacting so much from an already impoverished people. And the nation as a whole is spending more than what it earns.

If we add to the economic scenario the pressure of a rapidly growing population with its demands on our limited and dwindling resources, then we are in for an uphill struggle.

Indeed, a realistic appraisal of our present situation says that we are living in the worst of times. But this does not mean that we have to start digging foxholes. Something can still be done. We can overcome the crisis.

As Rizal said through Padre Florentino in *El Filibusterismo*, salvation presupposes sacrifice, sacrifice presupposes virtue, and virtue presupposes love. The redemption of the nation from its unfortunate situation is not just the task and the responsibility of government alone. The difficult and herculean task of repairing a nation in shambles falls squarely on the shoulder of every concerned Filipino. The accomplishment of this most challenging mission entails a slow, painful and collective process requiring no less than the patriotism, the nobility, and the idealism of all sectors of society.

Underpinning all our efforts to push the country forward is a strong sense of nationhood. If we allow ourselves to be guided purely by narrow sectoral interests, then we revert to a previous state as a cluster of islands divided by differences. Divided, there is nothing much we can achieve. But united in spirit and direction, everything is possible.

No people anywhere, anytime became great without first unifying their aspirations and integrating all their efforts. The histories of the Americans, the Japanese, the Chinese, the Germans, the French, the Italians, the Israelis, and the Singaporeans, to cite a few examples, prove what national unity can do. With a sense of nationhood, we are prepared to rise above our personal interests for the sake of our nation. We are willing to carry our share of the nation's burden. The little things we do when seen in the context of what is good for the country become an integral part of the process of nation building.

National unity is not alien to us. In fact, there were great moments in our past when we spoke with one voice and acted with a single purpose. The 1896 Revolution was not an isolated fire ignited by Tagalogs alone. It was a wider conflagration fueled by the outrage of a nation newly born.

From that consciousness of fighting a common foe, of living for common ideals, and of sharing common memories and dreams emerged vivid symbols of our sense of oneness. The emblem of our nationhood was conceived and unfurled. The notes that echo the love for the motherland were put together and sung.

When the first republic that we established was suppressed by another colonial power, we rallied behind the Filipino flag and fought with all our might as one nation. Much later when another aggressor came to take away our land, we stood united in defense of our honor and freedom.

That sense of nationhood that welded us together in times of trials now hangs precariously in the balance. Some of our brothers in Mindanao want to put up a separate and distinct state. Our compatriots in Cebu resent the use of Tagalog as the national language. If these centrifugal forces are not tamed by a larger unifying factor, what is left of the Filipino nation will be a relic of the past.

What Quezon had done for the country can be a refreshing reminder that there is, as there must be, a way out of the deepening shadows. In our time, we must in concert find a path to our future. With a sense of oneness, we shall get there.

A SUN IN THE CLOUDS

THERE is an unprecedented convergence of events that seriously puts to a test our collective capacity for survival and growth as a nation.

The full impact of the Persian Gulf crisis as it relates to our oil inventory level and the inward remittances of Filipino overseas contract workers based in the Middle East has been sending shock waves to the economy. Even before Iraq's invasion of Kuwait, there were already clear signals of a deepening economic crisis as manifested by a growing budgetary deficit, a continuing decline in the balance-of-payments position, an erosion in the value of the peso, and an upsurge in interest rates. Two natural calamities, the drought and the earthquake, conspired to add some more to our self-imposed burden.

Except for World War II, no other period in our history was as critically painful as the present. Certain life-styles have to be radically changed. To many, the question is not anymore a reduction in the level of comfort but sheer survival.

Those adversely affected by all these economic disturbances can deplore government's handling of state affairs. One can very well question fiscal and monetary policies. Or bewail structural imbalances in the economy. Or lament the unceasing dependence on imports.

Indeed, the problem has been analyzed repeatedly as to its causes. The next step is to make a serious attempt to change the status quo with something better. And this will require an understanding of the various forces that tend to obstruct the whole process as well as an intimate appreciation of the many factors that can bring about the desired future.

Cynics will mention some traits that frustrate the resolution of any crisis. The lack of a sense of urgency and the divisiveness in society are deadweights that prevent the ship of state from sailing forward. But these attitudinal stumbling blocks to progress can be pushed aside, as in fact they were sidelined at some points in the past, when national interest so demands. The organization of the Katipunan and the launching of the Filipino Revolution against Spain in the 1890s were historic events marked by a courageous resolve and an expansion of national consciousness. The reconstruction of the nation from the ruins of the last war was achieved with purpose and unity. And the peaceful revolution at EDSA demonstrated the Filipino people's oneness in winning back their freedom soonest.

At great moments in our history, we had enough sense of urgency and unity to pursue basic national ideals. This present crisis whose dark clouds loom above us is no exception. No nation on record has ever become prosperous without passing through a tunnel of adversity. Any crisis when collectively perceived as a challenge to national survival can revive and strengthen a people's ability to rise above their limitations.

In our worry about the shadow cast by the gathering clouds, we may forget that there is a sun that never fails to give light. As one high school student once wrote: "If you cry for missing the sun, your tears will prevent you from seeing the stars."

Truly, if we take stock of our strengths as a people, we have what it takes not only to survive but also to move forward. We are a very prayerful nation. In times of adversity, a nation in communion with God will never be abandoned. It is the very core of our Christian faith to believe that God in His mercy will never try us beyond our capacity to endure.

For all the injuries we have brought upon our environment, nature continues to yield its bounties for us to enjoy. We do not have all the oil that we need so we have to buy it from others. But we grow our own food. That makes a lot of difference.

We are noted in the region for our world-class managerial talents. Our social, political, and economic institutions while pressured by demographic expansion and by growing public expectations are intact and functioning.

Two recent sociological developments deserve special mention. The peaceful restoration of democracy which antedated the democratization of Eastern Europe is an eloquent proof of the Filipino people's high degree of political maturity. This national obsession with and commitment to democratic ideals creates a fertile ground for the flowering of the creative spirit. Human creativity is the driving force behind prosperity.

We may not give it much thought but the increasing interaction between the government and nongovernment people's groups on an institutional basis covering a wide area of common concerns strongly suggests synergistic initiatives. When ordinary folks assume responsibility for their future and when government is infused with a pro-people orientation, then no crisis is insurmountable.

We shall overcome.

A GARDEN IN MARIKINA

SIMPLE and ordinary people in their unaffected way have in various times shown their innate ability to make the most of what they have to create something new. This observation is confirmed by a quiet change process that is taking place in a school in Parang, Marikina.

A vegetable garden is verdant and vibrant in Fugoso Memorial School which is more popularly known as Boys Town. In this unassuming place, the school principal, the teachers, the pupils, and their parents have transformed the empty and barren piece of land within the campus into vegetable plots that are not far behind those found in Trinidad Valley which are managed commercially.

Admittedly, all vegetable gardens when carefully nurtured are alike. But this particular garden in Boys Town is unique. It has an inspiring story to tell—how the patience and dedication of an old man, a gardener at heart, has made gardeners out of so many.

Mr. Derpo, the principal, long before the "Gulayan Sa Paaralan" project was conceived by the Department of Agriculture was already a firm believer in school gardening. His childhood memories are those of the family farm and work animals in Sorsogon.

But this natural inclination towards the soil was not enough to make the school's garden plots yield healthy produce. In December of last year, the schoolground was predominantly brown with the negligible presence of sickly looking verdure. The impression was that not many teachers and pupils cared enough about planting vegetables. Seeds had to be bought out of meager school fund. The soil lacked nutrients.

All that the school in Boys Town needed was a little help in terms of vegetable seeds and technical assistance. The principal lost no time in getting initial inputs from Region IV of the Department of Agriculture when he heard of the "Gulayan Sa Paaralan" project in December. DA sent its project director together with an agri-technician to Boys Town. A number of field visits and consultations followed. The spadework and the quiet efforts have produced dramatic results.

Many lessons can be learned from the Boys Town experiment. When schoolchildren wake up early in the morning to gather livestock waste with which to condition and enrich their respective plots, when even parents join their children in tending the vegetable gardens, when every teacher starts feeling and believing that gardening for the pupils helps mould their character, when the people of the surrounding community seek to replicate what they see in Boys Town, then real transformation is taking place. And this is the dream of every change agent.

No amount of carefully conceived project with the most catchy slogan will be accepted and appreciated by its intended recipients if it is imposed and introduced with all the media blitz. The likelihood of an idea being perceived as another "pakulo" is ever present. So perceived, an idea will wither in the fleeting heat of *ningas cogon.*

An idea is accepted only when those with whom it is meant to be shared see themselves in it.

A QUIET TRANSFORMATION

IN many human settlements throughout the country, the pressure of population growth has intensified the strain on available life-sustaining resources. This is more graphically so among coastal fishing communities.

Without regard for the future, destructive fishing practices have been resorted to for convenience and instant gains. Mangrove areas have been destroyed in their conversion to fishpond estates. Unbridled industrial activities have contributed largely to the pollution and siltation of inland waters.

Nature could only react with a vengeance. The shortsightedness of some have impaired the marine ecosystem and caused a decline in the fish stocks of coastal waters. Panguil Bay in northwestern Mindanao is a classic example. From a production level of 2,578 metric tons in 1985, Panguil Bay's yield was down to 1,056 metric tons in 1987. In 1989 total output dropped further to 662 metric tons.

To the more than 5,000 fishermen in the 78 barangays of the provinces of Misamis Occidental, Zamboanga del Sur, and Lanao del Norte which bound the 18,000-hectare Panguil Bay, the continuing depletion of their immediate marine resources is too alarming. A critical point has been reached.

Barangay, municipal, and provincial officials together with affected fishing families and concerned civic groups took serious note. Years of indifference and neglect bowed to the message of survival. The need to survive caused a heightened ecological awareness. Advocates of environmental protection could not have found a more receptive audience.

The presence of a strong political will in the local leaderships, the painstaking process of community organizing, the many consultations among local officials, government line agencies, research institutions and NGOs—all these contributed to the growing collective concern to save Panguil Bay. Change has been institutionalized.

Overseeing the locally initiated multisectoral movement to bring back the bountiful marine life is the Panguil Bay Development Council. A product of local initiative, patience, vision and practicality, the council's chairmanship is rotated among the three governors. What makes this mechanism for inter-province cooperation unique is the fact that the provinces involved belong to separate regional jurisdictions.

A tri-sectoral task force serves as the operating arm of the council to synchronize all efforts at the rehabilitation and the long-term development of Panguil Bay.

To its credit, the Panguil Bay Development Council is the most active and results-oriented participant in the Fisheries Sector Program of the Department of Agriculture. Its vigorous campaign against illegal and destructive fishing methods has produced tangible results. There has been a noticeable increase in the catch of municipal fisherman. Moreover, several species of fish have returned into the bay.

In addition to the sustained law enforcement drive, fish sanctuaries have been identified in Tambulig, Zamboanga del Sur and in the Hulao-Hulao shoal in Ozamis City. Plans for 11 artificial reef complexes in 9 sites within the bay have been completed. Twelve municipalities are in the process of formulating zonation schemes for mangrove forests and aquatic resources.

Likewise, 96 fishermen's associations have been organized in preparation for various alternative livelihood assistance projects. Already, there are within the Panguil Bay coastal areas ten demonstration farms for the mariculture of seaweeds, grouper, milkfish and "siganid."

A quiet transformation is taking place in Panguil Bay.

THE FUTURE FOR FARMERS

THE Filipino farmer is poor. His poverty is an embarrassment to a society that is supposed to be the showcase of democracy's rebirth.

Where two-thirds of the country's population are rural-based, it is disturbing to note that more than one-half of rural families live below the level of marginal existence. Some 2.2 million rural families are in the bottom third of the income scale. In 1989 a rural family earned only an average income of P2,041 a month which was 25 percent lower than the poverty line of P2,700 previously defined by NEDA.

Moreover, a large number of farm families seriously suffer from malnutrition. According to the 1982 survey of the Food and Nutrition Research Institute, two-fifths of the farming community and more than one-third of fishermen could not afford adequate nutrition or 80 percent of the required energy intake.

A number of reasons may be cited for such a glaring proof of social injustice. The continuing poverty of the Filipino farmer is deeply rooted in structures and attitudes that are anti-people. The feudal legacy from a colonial past is still very much around. Real economic power continues to be within the exclusive hold of a select few. And the consequent political power is similarly controlled by an oligarchy.

Another constraint on the farmer's ability to improve his life is the long standing bias against agriculture as reflected in many public policy pronouncements and previous development strategies. There has been a marked preference for industrialization at the expense of agriculture. The NIC fixation has created an illusion that the country can be like Taiwan or South Korea by taking the industrial route. Not much thought is given to the fact that the industrial achievements of these two "tiger" economies are premised on a solid and dynamic agricultural base.

It is bad enough that a majority of our farmers and fishermen are poor. What makes the situation even more alarming is the reduction of hectarage devoted to agriculture coupled with the depletion of our land and marine resources. Meanwhile, the subsistence orientation of farmers persists.

Paradoxically, it is the disadvantaged agricultural sector that can propel the economy to its growth targets. When its full potential is realized, a sizable purchasing power can be generated to strengthen the local market. A vibrant countryside can lure back some of its people who have moved over to urban centers in search of a living.

What does it take then to emancipate the farmer from despair? As true of every quest process, there is a need for a clear and compelling vision. The Filipino farmer will always be a prisoner of his past unless he learns to see himself in an expanded role in a new environment. He cannot forever be at the mercy of factors and forces beyond his control. He must look at his life as more than a tedious process of keeping body and soul together. Planting rice can be fun if the farmer can add new values to his effort, if he is able to minimize his risk by exerting a measure of influence on the market, and if he has easy access to affordable credit facilities and post-harvest assistance.

This vision of a new breed of farmer-entrepreneurs who can do profitable business in dynamic rural communities is indeed too good to be true. But it is being translated into action in many parts of the country. A quiet revolution is taking place outside the wall of the city. Farmers are beginning to realize that they can do much more.

Government cannot afford to be outside the mainstream of this historic reawakening. If only for the fact that the majority of the Filipino people are farmers and fishermen, the government has the moral and constitutional duty to improve their productivity, increase their real incomes, and uplift the quality of their lives.

If the government is deeply concerned about the future of Filipino farmers and fishermen, then at the policy level it can manifest its commitment by carving out a long-term sustainable development program that transcends narrow political interests. This means a drift away from shortsighted subsidies and other unimaginable and counterproductive systems of doleout. A more meaningful and lasting government intervention would be in terms of efficient service delivery systems covering research and extension, credit, irrigation, storage, processing, and transportation, among other things.

Not all the infrastructure support can do much if the whole bureaucracy behind is not imbued with a pro-people and service-oriented work ethic. Only those who truly care about people, about Filipinos as brothers will give their best to help them.